HOW TO BECOME A CHAMPION

AT

BOWLS

AN ACCEPTED TEXT BOOK, IN GREATER DEMAND
THAN ANY TREATISE EVER WRITTEN ON THE
GAME

_____

A COMPLETE COURSE OF MODERN INSTRUCTION
(ILLUSTRATED)

_____

COMPILED BY THE LATE R. T. HARRISON
(For many years, Editor of Sydney 'Referee' Bowls page)
and incorporating
'ETIQUETTE OF BOWLS' by the late J. P. MONRO, B.A.
'ETIQUETTE OF MARKING' by the late JOHN A. MALAN
and
'THE ROMANCE OF BOWLS MANUFACTURE'
by the late J. P. MONRO, B.A.

_____

Published by
R. W. HENSELL & SONS PTY. LTD.
16 Wreckyn Street, North Melbourne, Victoria 3051
Australia

ISBN 0 9597152 0 7

1st Edition	1939	10th Edition	1957
2nd Edition	1946	11th Edition	1958
3rd Edition	1948	12th Edition	1960
4th Edition	1950	13th Edition	1964
5th Edition	1951	14th Edition	1969
6th Edition	1953	15th Edition	1975
7th Edition	1954	16th Edition	1976
8th Edition	1955	17th Edition	1983
9th Edition	1956	18th Edition	1986

Wholly set up, printed and bound by
The Dominion Press-Hedges & Bell
Maryborough 3465

PUBLISHERS' PREFACE TO 18TH EDITION

SINCE 'How to Become a Champion at Bowls' was first published, the game and laws of lawn bowls have had many changes and whilst recent changes have rendered obsolete some aspects of the Author's theories, the essential basic theories advocated by the colourful (and sometimes controversial) old champion remain and form the basis of many top bowlers' games today.

It is most regrettable that owing to 'Dick' Harrison having passed on, he could not completely up-date what is the biggest selling and most widely read and quoted book on lawn bowls, but that his theories still apply is testimony to his writings and the command he had of the game.

To give what we consider to be the most complete coverage of lawn bowls yet put together in one volume, we have added to Harrison's writings—'The Etiquette of Bowls' and 'The Romance of Bowls Manufacture' both by the late J. P. Monro, B.A. (a former Secretary of the Royal Victorian Bowls Association and noted bowls historian) and 'The Etiquette of Marking' by the late John A. Malan (a former Life Member of the Royal Victorian Bowls Association) who undertook the task of re-editing and revising where necessary, the 14th edition when the Australian Bowls Council adopted the use of the small mat which is standard in other countries.

We also gratefully acknowledge the assistance of the late Len Richards (Warrawee Bowls Club, NSW) in the preparation of the fifteenth and sixteenth editions.

Although written for Australian conditions, the principles in this volume apply generally to most countries where lawn bowls are played and we believe this edition has a usefulness far beyond any previous edition and will be welcomed by bowlers everywhere.

R. W. Hensell & Sons Pty Ltd

LIST OF ILLUSTRATIONS

CONTENTS

ABOUT THE AUTHOR

THE Author, R. T. 'Dick' Harrison was born at Dunolly (Victoria) on 14th December, 1872 and after serving in the Boer War, joined the Carlton Bowls Club in Melbourne during October 1903.

Shortly afterwards, he transferred to the neighbouring club, Victoria, and this move set the pattern of his bowls career for 50 years because, in that time he was involved in more than 15 transfers between clubs in two states—often with an air of mystery and/or controversy surrounding them.

There are several gaps in his career when he completely dropped out of bowls and although there is not a complete record of his performances available, what is still recorded speaks for itself—particularly when you consider he won the Single Handed Championship of Victoria after having been bowling for only 2 years and 4 months, followed by 9 club and 3 state championships in 17 years. When he won the Victorian Champion of Champions title in 1943 at 70 years of age, it was 36 years after he first won the same title and at the age of 75, he captained the four that won the N.S.W. title in 1947.

Some highlights of his career were:

In Victoria

Carlton Bowling Club
1903   Joined the Club

Victoria Bowling Club
1906   Won Club Championship
1906   Runner-up State Champion of Champions
1906   Won State Singles Championship
1907   Won Club Championship
1907   Won State Champion of Champions

Auburn Bowling Club
1908   Won Club Championship
1908   Runner-up State Singles Championship
1909   Won Club Championship

Hawthorn City Bowling Club
1910   Won Club Championship
1911   Won Consolation Singles at Australian Bowls Council Carnival—Adelaide

Alma Bowling Club
1914   Won Club Championship

Glenhuntly Bowling Club
1915   Won Club Championship
1918   Won Club Championship

Canterbury Bowling Club
1919   Won State Fours Championship (Skip)
1920   Won Club Championship

In New South Wales

1923   Became Editor of Sydney 'Referee' bowls page writing under by-line of 'Boomerang'

Waverley Bowling Club
1926 Reached Club Championship final, but the match was awarded to his opponent

North Sydney Bowling Club
1932 Won Sydney Harbour Bridge Fours Carnival (Skip)
1932 Runner-up Sydney Harbour Bridge Singles Carnival

Hunters Hill Bowling Club
1933 Won Club Championship
1933 Won State Pairs Championship (Skip)
1933 Won Metropolitan Fours Championship (Skip)
1933 Won State Fours Championship (Skip)
1935 Won State Singles Championship
1936 Won Australian Pairs Championship at Australian Bowls Council Carnival in Perth
1937 Won Club Championship
1937 Won Metropolitan Pairs Championship (Skip)
1937 Won State Pairs Championship (Skip)

Victoria Park Bowling Club
1939 Won Club Championship
1940 Won Club Championship
1941 Won Club Championship

In Victoria

Moreland Bowling Club
1942 Runer-up State Veteran Singles Championship
1943 Won Club Championship
1943 Won State Champion of Champions

Carlton Bowling Club
1945 Won State Veteran Pairs Championship (Skip)

In New South Wales

Victoria Park Bowling Club
1947 Won State Fours Championship (Skip)

In Victoria

1947 Re-joined Hawthorn City (now City of Hawthorn) Bowling Club
1951 Joined Dunolly Bowling Club

The last known appearance of 'Dick' Harrison in a major tournament was when he skipped a composite four of Victorians in the Australian Bowls Council Carnival in Sydney in 1953 and reached the quarter-finals of the fours championship. He was then 80 years of age. He died in Melbourne in 1956.

DIGNIFIED ATMOSPHERE OF BOWLS

THROUGHOUT all the years there have been men playing the game of bowls who, despite the milestones that would remind them that they were 'not as young as they used to be,' never really grew old. Many such are with us to-day, and the future will bring no change.

The Divine Plan demands that all shall cross the Bar sooner or later, and most old bowlers, in their periods of peaceful solitude, have given thanks for a pastime that has made the way not so weary.

The dignity of the ancient sport, the pure atmosphere that it creates among those who follow it, will ever be an infallible tonic that will preserve the sentiment expressed in the opening pages of this treatise.

INTRODUCTION

SPORT may be defined as an irresistible magnet that not merely attracts, but grips like a vyce all the human fragments within its powerful influence. It is an antidote for all the ills that mankind is subject to, and provides depots in every city, town, and village.

But sport has to be treated with tenderness and respect for its dignity and virtues. Expose it to organised commercialism and it is liable to become a dangerous and degrading plague.

Many thousands of bowlers have good cause to offer up thanks for an avenue of relaxation and social intercourse that does not bring depression of soul and financial commitments in its trail. Assuredly, the bowling green is not only the nursery of restraint against human weaknesses, but the headquarters of clean, untrammelled and health-giving sport.

The game of bowls to-day is an entirely different proposition from what it had previously been, and is now more readily taken up by a younger generation, which hitherto regarded it as a pastime solely for men of mature years.

Outstanding reason why 75 per cent of the bowlers of to-day are 'just bowlers' is, in the opinion of the author, due to the fact that no system has been forthcoming by which the student might be guided; no gradual process of education, but rather a cart-before-the-horse procedure that makes him one of the great army that never rise above mediocrity.

One of the most intricate, if not the most intricate, game to become efficient at, bowls must be systematised. Strong emphasis should be laid against the student going on to a green until he has moulded himself by a study of 'combination,' or system, and is thoroughly conversant with the outstanding principles. I take the view, emphatically, that nobody who has not reached the highest pinnacle in the field, who cannot demonstrate on the green the doctrines he propounds, can be accepted as an authority, and lay down methods for guidance of others.

In this connection I originated the 'homework' aspect, counselling the beginner to strictly refrain from going on to a green for some time after beginning a study of the treatise. Combination is, in reality, a chain of things to be learnt, taken link by link, until the student becomes a machine in spite of himself. We are all creatures of habit, and it is just as easy to acquire good habits as bad ones, and much more beneficial.

Nothing can be more conclusive than actual demonstration, and the author has for many years demonstrated the soundness of his doctrines in the field, the only place that should be acceptable to the keen critic. While there can be many and varied wrong methods of holding or gripping a bowl, of standing on the mat, and in other directions vital to success, I claim that the methods herein propounded, particularly in the matters of grip and stance, are the ones that will give best results.

Psychology is still far from the exact science that bowling is becoming through genius and perseverance. Someone defined genius as: 'An infinite capacity for taking pains.' Nevertheless, some of the broad principles governing the functioning of mind are now well recognised, and they apply to bowling as they do to every action in human life, whether the bowler knows it or not.

Let us take a common incident which well illustrates the effect of mental attitude on bowling. A bowl stops a yard short 'in the draw.' Any experienced player knows that no one bowl, more than a foot from the jack, can actually block a draw shot: by slightly changing one's position on the mat, it is always possible to get either inside or outside the block. Yet the man who says to himself, 'That's dead in my way,' is almost sure to crash into it. Another man says, 'That is an excellent guide,' and he is confident he can just miss it and get a perfect shot. Although few are aware of it, these little things which we say to ourselves, in other words our thoughts, have a tremendous influence on our actions.

Now, I must impress on you that, whether you intend it or not, you cannot help constantly making auto-suggestions to your sub-conscious mind, and that your every thought about bowling has its own tiny effect on your game, the aggregate effect of the total being incredibly great. What you *can* help is the general trend of your thoughts, whether they assist or

3

impede your development along the lines laid down in this book. The men who have not patience or perseverance enough to practise Combination, until they have fixed it in their 'habit minds,' will not be the only ones who fail to get the improvement in their play, which is there to be dug out.

The man who thinks he can 'never adopt the changed stance at my age,' and he who tells himself that the Elevation Theory is 'too deep for me,' will never fully master the new methods. Personally I have been working on the 'Combination' long enough to have made every movement automatic, as far as possible.

You must be careful to deny forcibly any negative thought that you will never succeed or that you cannot master this or that, and also take care that you phrase every mental statement in a form acceptable to reason. Note also that you can make the suggestion either general, playing better or particular to the special factor in the Combination which you are working on at the time—draw, grip, stance, delivery, etc. The surprising value of the instructions for home practice results from their making the several movements habitual.

Another very successful method of applying auto-suggestion is by making mental pictures, in this case of yourself carrying out the Combination in full detail. Visualise yourself on the mat; see the rink with the jack at the other end; estimate its distance; *see* the curve your bowl must take to rest on it, and yourself gripping the bowl, thumb on crown, fingers behind as the book instructs. *See* yourself assuming the correct stance and elevating the bowl an exact height; see the right arm swing back and then the left foot step forward the determined distance, and the right knee bend to the necessary angle and the arm swing forward in a smooth, simultaneous, uniform delivery, releasing the bowl and following through with the palm upward.

Make yourself hold the picture of the completed swing, and watch the bowl curl right in and rest on the jack. Make every detail complete and as vivid as possible; if you can *feel* it as well as see it, so much the better. Then repeat with the other three bowls, and picture them all clustered round the jack, so that a handkerchief would cover the lot.

This is an excellent method, which will help many more

than the one mentioned previously. I believe that which of the two ways suits the individual better depends on whether he is 'eye-minded' or 'ear-minded.' Do you easily remember the gist of a lecture, or do you find that reading and studying illustrations is more useful to fix a subject in your mind? Find that out and you have the best guide as to which method to make use of. A mental picture, formed vividly just before you drop off to sleep, will be working in the sub-conscious through the night.

If you follow instructions in the positive mental attitude indicated above, anticipating and recognising each bit of improvement as it develops, you will benefit to a much greater degree in less time.

One more thought on the psychology of bowling. We often hear it said: 'Oh, So-and-so will never get anywhere; he's a splendid bowler, but he hasn't the temperament.' Other good bowlers are said not to have the right temperament to make good skippers. The deficiencies of such men are not physical but mental.

Those who have the positive temperament naturally are fortunate, but, just as I insist that bowlers can be made, so can those who are affected with an inferiority complex overcome it and build up the champion's temperament by the use of auto-suggestion. Perhaps the best definition of temperament ever given was: 'The sum of a man's fixed habits of thought.' Bowling is a microcosm of life; if you wish to become a bowling champion, you must control and direct your bowling thoughts.

As a final caution, I would advise you not to permit doubts to take root in your mind as to whether some other grip, stance, or anything different might not suit you better than mine. Men have won, and will continue to win, distinction in our sport who do not follow my ideas in full. I claim that my grip, stance, etc. are the perfect ones; and I do insist, by virtue of my record, that they are the best, and that each fits in with the other to form a Combination by which I have taught *thousands* to make themselves first-class in a strikingly short period. I teach a tested, scientific, and inclusive Combination. You have to supply perseverance, confidence and thoroughness; as you sow, you will surely reap.

5

IF THE BOWL COULD TALK

WHEN you pick up the first of your four bowls to begin a match, the bowl would say, if it could talk:

'Do the correct thing by me and put me on the right track, and I will do the rest.'

Successive bowls would say the same, but you might ask: 'What do you mean by "correct things" and "the right track"?'

'Well, you lay the mat, throw the jack, and pick up that first bowl.' No need to tell you that it is a dead, brainless and non-co-operating thing.

It can neither hear, speak, nor do what is expected of it unless the operator possesses complete knowledge of the essentials that bring about desired results.

The first of a number of correct things the operator must do is to get into sympathy with and infuse life into that dead thing you expect so much of.

The player at this initial stage calls his brain power into action, and it in turn instructs such player to use the soft, first-joint, fleshy points of the fingers and thumb to feel the surface of the bowl.

It calls upon the nerves running to the points of the fingers and thumb to operate in such a manner that the player and the bowl come into sympathy.

That is why time should be taken at this early stage so that the delivery should not be premature.

So many players 'go off half-cock,' and thus, if the bowl could remonstrate, it would surely say:

'How can you expect me to do a job if you don't make me part of it, concentrate, and send me away with judgment and ease?'

But assuming that care and concentration are not missing, there are other considerations.

Delay and concentration on length and green bring touch into the picture.

While getting the feel of the bowl, and resultant touch, the player must grip, or hold it, the right way.

That right way with many is the wrong way, and all bowls held with the thumb at the side is the wrong way.

He must stand balanced, and hold the bowl six inches

below the elbow, after his arms are held out naturally in front.

He must bend over his work at the same angle as a batsman at cricket, or a putter at golf.

He must step out with his leg so as to do so with the swing forward of his bowling arm. That means correct and rythmical timing, which is one of the big essentials.

If he does all these things, he is doing exactly what the bowl would ask him to do, could it speak.

It all means something else. A perfectly moulded physical condition, and there only remains attention to good length play, and the operator must show out well.

The 'something else' also includes control. Most bowls control the players.

Play by rule of thumb, system, and to figures, and you must have a lot on the opposition.

EARLY CAUTION AND THE SEQUEL

ONE of the most interesting of the thousands of communications the author has received, ran in part:

'You write much, from time to time, about "blowing into the game," by which I take to mean wrong approach. I am sure it would help many who are being tossed on the high seas of uncertainty if you would describe just how you came in, as it must have been by the right door.'

The reply was:

When my decision was made that the game was worthwhile, I did nothing for a time, beyond visiting several greens where leading players were to be seen in action, and studying their methods.

Noting that all appeared to be a law unto themselves, I decided upon doing the same. No two were alike, either in respect of grip, stance, or delivery. Nobody could give an intelligent answer to queries as to what were correct methods, hence the decision.

For a year I was a lonely figure, 'working out,' discovering, or persevering until satisfied, then standardising for permanent use. That my approaches were correct was amply demonstrated, for all championships fell to me in turn, when in the second year I decided to display my 'wares.'

Of course, one had to run the gauntlet of much good-natured banter and ridicule, but practice of the methods adopted (which I have not changed after 48 years) convinced me that nobody can just 'blow in,' and succeed by emulating the 98 per cent he sees around him. Taking each department of the game, and exploiting it in turn, about sums up the position.

If, then, the man who would be something out of the ordinary carries out to the letter the instructions contained in the following pages, there is no logical reason why he should not gain the highest honours.

As in my case, restraint against the urge from well-meaning friends to get into the game prematurely has to be exercised. It is entirely in the hands of the man himself.

CHOOSING A MODEL

COMING to a decision as to what line of action the newcomer to the game should take, with a view to a career, must be left to the individual himself. It is a decision that should not be arrived at hurriedly, and the purpose of this brief annotation is to assist those setting out on this momentous expedition.

Following or imitating leading successful players cannot be entirely recommended, despite the fact that achievement is a first pointer to recommendation. There are so many and such a variety of men who have attained to the Classics and continue to show out, that the student would find difficulty in his final choice.

Quite frankly, I would say that the great percentage of successful players, being a law unto themselves, and no two alike, constitute a problem for the beginner very difficult of solution. The Alpha and Omega of good bowling are the possession and control of the correct movements.

What is meant by 'correct movements'? Surely the proper method of holding the bowl, standing or poising, so that all the muscles of the body, and not merely portion of them, are employed, stepping out as Nature teaches us to walk and carrying out the whole as one action.

If the greens are visited for the purpose of discovering one of these all-correct actionists, only a very limited number will be found. It may be put forward that if the beginner models his game on that of a current State Championship winner, for instance, he would be justified.

Not by any means necessarily! Then, it might be asked, why should the seeker after a career follow the methods propounded in the pages of this treatise?

Answering for ourselves, we would plead: This is the eighteenth edition of an essay on the game that has stood the test of time, produced thousands of high-class players, and has been the accepted textbook. Yet the great decision still remains with the beginner as to whom he should follow. How will he exercise his judgment?

If every bowler could, in rotation, sit in front of a screen, and see just how all the rest acted—how they gripped, how they stood on the mat, and the thousand and one different methods of greening the bowl—they would be amazed. The first question asked by any one of them would be: 'Why are they nearly all different?'

The career of a bowler, for good or ill, depends wholly and solely upon his approach to the game. The initiation period for the bowler is his most critical, for he is going to be either spoilt or put on the right track.

Who are to spoil him, and who are to put him on the right track? Who, outside of himself, is competent to say what he should or should not do, whom he should consult, upon whom to model his game? That is where his, and the real, trouble begins.

What actually happens to the great majority is this: A number of clubs have their coaches. Into the hands of these the newcomer falls, again for good or ill. Almost invariably it is ill. No two teach or instruct alike. Ninety-five per cent of the club coaches I have seen are incompetent, some pitifully so. All take their charges out to the green straight away, instead of first moulding them indoors.

The best proof of this is the annual showdown in any club you can name. If there is a correct way of playing billiards, golf, cricket, bowls, anything, then there cannot be fifty correct ways. But if you name fifty bowling club coaches you name fifty different ways. Therefore, the student must be particularly careful about this early approach to the game.

If you are going off on an extended tour, to somewhere you have never been before, you very carefully consult experts as to where and to how you are going, what risks you run, etc. How exceedingly careful you should be, then, in taking this 'long trip' which will constitute your bowling career, the pitfalls that it entails, and the ruination that it may bring to all your hopes?

Well-Meaning Friends?

The difficulty is to determine what are the correct methods, who propounds them, and who are to be the determiners. At the moment the student has to rely either on his own poor judgment, or accept the advice of well-meaning friends or club coaches.

Taking newcomers and putting them into games of any kind in the first weeks of their initiation is to exterminate all chance of their ever being anything but 'just bowlers.'

There are many good players who would be good under any conditions; but pass their methods on to a pupil, and an entirely different result follows. In short, there is an open road to success. It must be a systematised, standardised, streamlined, dovetailed method in which brain, muscle and nerve co-operate to one common end.

If anyone should feel sceptical about the existence of such a multiplicity of faulty modes and methods, as is repeatedly said to exist by the compiler of this work, he can very speedily be brought to a realisation of the position by the simple process of a visit to any green where a match is in progress.

Indeed, such a check has been made on many occasions, when students have been in hand, with a view of demonstrating to them where they would probably finish without approaching the game correctly, and being properly trained.

When 16 fours, or 64 players, are functioning on one green, and no two are found to be alike, that is the best evidence of the lack of a universally practised method of teaching. The matter contained in the following pages is possibly the best lead-up to what the newcomer must do if he desires to succeed.

Self-examination occasionally is a sure line to your progress or otherwise. Put your mental chart into black and white and see how you stand. 'I think I have deteriorated' is a compulsory pill, if sometimes a bitter one.

If you be termed 'a crank,' give yourself a pat on the back, for mostly the crank is a problem when it comes to a showdown.

Think for yourself in all things bowls, but never be ashamed to take a leaf from the other chap's experience. The man who knows 'all there is to know' about the game is usually the easiest to beat.

STANDARDISE EVERYTHING

SYSTEM is practised in almost everything, and certainly should be, in order to become proficient in sport.

No game calls for systematic procedure more than bowls. The common trend is to slip along haphazardly, with disastrous results to the student's career. Each subject must be approached separately and thoroughly exploited.

The human element in bowls can never attain the precision of a machine, but it can be trained to such a degree of proximity that the difference is not so very marked.

I say quite definitely that if the student or would-be improver standardises the movements that I have practised over the years he can achieve similar results to mine.

The present-day follower is much better catered for than his predecessors. Ill-shaped bowl curiosities of former times have practically disappeared from the greens, and wood has been replaced by more reliable and durable material.

Standardised shape, weight, size and administrative control in eliminating undesirable practices, all assist toward a better game and increased interest. The incomer must march with the times, and exploit these advantages to the full.

Walking on to the mat and sending a second bowl up differently from the first, failing to dovetail the movements, or departing from the principles laid down, is not system.

Many who are taught improved methods slip back to bad habits because old-timers tell them not to do this or that. A little of each spells failure.

Approached from the right angle, the game of bowls is as simple to learn as ABC, but quite difficult to make headway with if taken haphazard.

Lay down a foundation, play by rule, and take the problems one by one, beginning with the bowl; and who can say bowls is a difficult game to learn?

The exclusive instructional contents of this treatise will set out how one can, by systematic application, reach the pinnacle of efficiency promised in its introductory remarks.

Wise in his generation will be the man who takes the Combination chain link by link, and does not fall to the urge to jump his obstacles before he comes to them.

Concentration upon laying a solid foundation, and devoting as much time as possible to those movements and methods that will lead him naturally into mastering the finer points later, must ever be kept in view.

TAKING THE GAME SERIOUSLY

SOONER or later you will have to decide whether you are a social or a competitive bowler. The question is often asked —mostly by incompetents—'Why take the game so seriously?' Is there anything worth while that is not worth taking seriously?

The author has ever propounded that all games can, and should, be played to the entire satisfaction of all by amalgamating the social and the competitive. Why not?

It is mostly propaganda from inefficients that it 'should not be taken too seriously.' You seldom, if ever, get such advice from the better players.

Unfortunately for its progress and welfare, raw novices find their way on to various associations as delegates all too easily.

They blossom forth on to committees, secure, rather than become elected to, positions as selectors, green committees, and other offices. They burlesque the game, hence their slogan: 'Don't take the sport too seriously.'

You, who come freshly into it, have the task imposed upon you of insisting that bowls be played in the spirit as displayed in Interstate matches— a fusion of the social and the competitive. Why not unite the two in all events?

Then the sport will progress still more rapidly and be accepted as something more than 'a pastime for men in their dotage' by other writers on sport ignorant of the subject.

IMPORTANCE OF CORRECT APPROACH

No game has been less correctly approached by the beginner than bowls. And often when it has been properly approached, the lack of a competent mentor has left him where he started.

Let us, then, take the student from the moment he is introduced as a prospective member of the club.

He meets the members, and is invariably taken straight into the game. That is to say, he is encouraged in doing what he is most eager to do himself, viz go out on to the green to see what sort of a fist he makes of it.

The unfortunate pupil is given a pair of shoes, and, with the very best intentions, handed over to the official coach, or, in his absence—and that is mostly the case— one who lends him a set or pair of bowls without regard to size or weight, after a guess as to the probable need.

The first fatal lesson, or demonstration, is his undoing. He may or may not be told how to hold the bowl correctly, and if they are too large he immediately adopts the wrong grip. He may or may not be told how to stand correctly on the mat, and so the first lesson of destruction goes on unchecked, his so-called mentor, meanwhile, assuming an air of satisfaction that he is more than doing his job.

That recruit thus joins the great army of 75 per cent, the ever-increasing number spoilt for all time in their toddling days. He has been vaccinated with the wrong serum, and instead of being able to withstand the 'diseases' that will surely envelop him, becomes a permanent cot case.

I would say to newcomers: Don't walk into a club and begin to play on top of your introduction as a member. Don't be persuaded by anyone to try your hand, no matter how strong the urge. Be content to stand on the bank, and decide what the game is about, and how, through the devious ways, you will eventually be able to get your bowls in close proximity and consistently around that white kitty.

There are many things essential to the beginner before he even steps on to a green for the first time, and in these initial remarks I include the man who is not too far gone in the incorrect methods sense. There are thousands of players in their first and second years, and with them it is by no means too late to undo faulty methods.

My contention is proved by the history of the game everywhere. Not even the most argumentative can deny that 75 per cent of bowlers are inefficient. Clubs find the utmost difficulty in getting together a good sixteen for pennants, and what is left over speaks all languages in the direction I indicate.

There must be some reason for this state of affairs. The reason is at hand: just what I have pointed out—the wrong method of approaching the game, and the subsequent disaster it brings in its train.

If there is any other reason, what is it?

'Correct approach' also embraces other important points for the beginner's education. On another page, the author mentions that he has frequently been called upon to send a pupil back, with instructions to remould his physical state or condition.

If you have played previously, but wrongly, your old state must be remodelled, and the muscles shifted to the proper places, in order to conform to the principles set out in the pages immediately following this article. It entails temporary soreness, which passes rapidly.

Getting the right bowl, holding it properly, standing in such position on the mat that all the muscles are brought into play, and not merely some of them, produces that perfect physical state, or condition, and the student at once becomes a rhythmical delivering machine.

He does not acquire a 'corporation,' and his balance improves with his new condition. Not until the desired physical state is acquired can the subject expect to make any headway.

I have frequently been approached with a view to bettering a player's game, and have been forced to tell the would-be improver that if he could absorb at once all that I could tell him about the methods for his advancement it would be quite a waste of effort and time.

To be able to work on a subject one has to be in the same position as a surgeon who informs his patient that before operating on him he must be prepared for the ordeal from the physical angle.

One of the most apt pupils to pass through my hands, and,

14

since then, one of the most successful playing the game, was a medical man. He conceded at the inception that he had wasted five years of his life employing wrong methods.

The first week of his tuition had the effect of creating a soreness, due to the gradual changing of the muscles from the wrong to the right quarter.

ASPIRING CHAMPION

IT cannot be too often stressed that the universal method of handling newcomers, or anyone seeking improvement, is entirely wrong here and overseas alike.

To take them out on to a green, set a jack and begin to teach them, borders not only on the ridiculous, but has a very bad psychological effect.

Persons so treated are exposed to the gaze of all and sundry, who peer at them through the pavilion windows, and the less tactful even stand round, listen and whisper criticism.

Anyone seeking improvement, no matter what his degree of skill, should be taken in hand indoors, reasoned with, and put through an examination.

An examination paper should be prepared for him and a mat laid down. He should be told to produce his actions in grip, stance, delivery, timing, in keeping with what he has been accustomed.

He is checked up and corrected on size of bowl, grip, stance, delivery, elevation, timing (on the fundamental side), and facing, firm shots, drives and timing of latter two—on the fine points side of chart.

After each action, the examiner makes an entry on the chart, but delays passing on the diagnosis until the faults are all made plain.

Correction follows demonstration, and at the termination of a couple of hours, the student, unlike the ones so grossly mishandled, looks and feels 100 per cent improved. He takes the coach's diagnosis home with him.

This process of moulding, and practising out the correct movements, is continued at home, there in evenings from a mat and on a carpet. In not one case have I seen anyone return (in a specified time) whose transformation has not been pleasing.

After a second visit (for re-examination) the subject then, and only then, is finished off on a green.

Of thousands taught on these lines by the author, over forty years, not one has ever come back on him—on the contrary.

It is pardonable to ask, therefore, why these ruination processes continued unchecked.

Follow these lines and there will never be any need for a course of *casus belli* courage drops.

RIGHT SIZE BOWL IS ESSENTIAL

GOOD bowling consists of getting consistently close to the objective, and, to be consistent, the aspiring champion must have some system to work upon.

In order to succeed, let me say, in defeating an opponent in a game of 31 up, and consistently doing it, a player has to act on a set policy of performing certain movements that dovetail into one another, and which I call Combination, or systematising your game.

For instance, it is quite useless getting the right bowl to suit the hand if you don't hold it correctly, and, by the same rule, what is the use of so holding it if your stance and balance are faulty? Therefore, you must get the Combination, or system, and work on it so that you will know no other, and therefore not fall into error.

I work the Combination from the moment I step on to the green, doing everything by rule, figures, and system. If I can succeed, why not you? In that 31 up you must be able to bring to bear upon it, through ever-changing positions, the whole set of things that form the systematisation of your game. It is a chain, and you cannot afford to have a weak link in it.

Just as a golf expert does not merely spread his feet out and swipe at the ball, without regard to approach, stance, swing, etc, then getting consistently around the kitty, and performing the numerous shots, is not accomplished without something akin to the system adopted by the golfer.

Imagine the futility of a beginner being taken on to a green and starting to play bowls in the absence of these preliminary explanations—is it any wonder he never gets anywhere?

16

The great army of bowlers have just drifted into the game, and inside of a week or two are found trying to do shots and performing acts that they should not have looked at until they have been initiated into, and conquered, the fundamental principles. He who exercises great patience and restraint cannot go wrong if he approaches the game in the manner laid down here.

It is necessary to cease dreaming of getting on to kitty, and to concentrate upon the initial essentials; to get the muscles of the arms and the rest of the body set into a permanent mould, so that when the more forward lessons are approached the pupil finds himself prepared to meet them.

And the next thing to concentrate upon is securing the bowl that suits the hand. A mercer sells many sizes in gloves because the demand comes from many sizes in hands. That is the position the bowler is in, and it is essential that he should be fitted aright.

That there is something in the relation of the bowl to the hand can be gathered from the fact that seven distinct sizes in bowls have been provided by experienced manufacturers. If everybody could handle the bigger sizes there would be no necessity for the smaller ones, or a variety of sizes.

The first thing the prospective champion must determine is to find out which particular size of the seven suits his hand best, always having regard to the grip.

In order to get the size of bowl, turn to Fig. 1 showing method in picture.

Pick up the bowl as often as the opportunity presents itself, and practise holding it, nothing else, just to form your hand muscles to its conformity, and wait till you get the next lesson before adopting a permanent grip. However, in this preliminary 'nursing' of the bowl, place the thumb anywhere between the rings and the running edge that is most comfortable. Don't on any account place the thumb on the disc side of the rings.

On the question of getting the essential article, it is amazing how many men continue to separate themselves from a higher standard and increased results by using bowls somebody sold as a bargain or numbered among the thousands of obsolete menaces that can only be described as cheap and nasty.

I insist that you get the best, and thus emulate every champion in every kind of sport. What that best amounts to is for you to decide after due consideration and scrutiny. A points-producing bowl is like a good car: it will save the owner much worry and get him there sooner.

Now, having secured the bowl that is related to your particular hand, you have forged the first link in the Combination chain, and begun with a system. Don't attempt any carpet or drawing-room delivery; don't do anything until you get your next lesson, which will be the best method of grip, and even then you will not be asked to do any stepping out. Later you will appreciate the reason for this early restraint.

HAND IN RELATION TO SIZE OF BOWL

MANY bowlers sacrifice control by using a bowl too large for the hand—the 'palm-sitters' are in this category and lose finger and thumb spin, which is one of the essentials. If the departure is made in order to secure weight, I would say the gain is not worth the other sacrifice.

A player should use the biggest (and heaviest) bowl you can most comfortably *hold* and *control* in your hand under all playing conditions likely to be encountered.

Other factors then come into the final selection, such as the moistness (or dryness) of the hand and the player's build and strength—all of which lead back to comfortably holding and controlling the bowl.

The gripping of the bowl in the manner illustrated (Fig. 1) to arrive at the correct size bowl to play with emanated from the Author and is a good guide to securing the correct size.

The method is to make the thumb nails meet first, then clamp the bowl tightly around the circumference until the tip of the longer finger just touches its opposite.

It is usually a sign that if a hand cannot make the longer fingers just meet around the circumference of a bowl, that particular bowl is too large for the hand—however, some players may perform this easily, but not be able to hold and control the bowl because of the continually moist (or dry) nature of their hands.

Players with very small hands must perforce use the Size 3 ($4\frac{7}{8}''$) or smaller sizes. It is fatal to attempt to control any bowl too large for the hand. Players who prefer the medium size, even though they are able to use the larger size, are not necessarily driven to adopt the larger size in order to obtain extra weight because of the range of sizes and weights now available.

ABOUT ROLLING THE JACK

SOME little things in bowls loom large, when they unexpectedly appear, and cause no end of consternation. It might, therefore, be just as well that we should be prepared for these contingencies, trifling as they may seem.

All scoring measurements in bowls are made from the nearest point of a bowl to the nearest point of the jack. However, except where the laws specifically state otherwise, any measurement from the middle of the front of the mat to the jack must be taken along the surface of the green to the point of contact with the green, as this is the 'true' position of a sphere on a plane surface.

For a 110-ft (33 m) green, the furthest point the front of the mat may be laid is 38 ft (11.5 m) from the rear ditch, to give a minimum length end. For a 120-ft (36.5 m) green it is 48 ft (15 m) and in the case of a 125-ft (38 m) green it would be 53 ft (16 m).

Take one of these as an example—the 120-ft (36.5 m) green. If the mat line be 48 ft (15 m) from the rear ditch and the jack 6 ft (2 m) from the front ditch, then the remaining distance would be 66 ft (20 m) or the minimum distance allowed.

I have found the following a good and safe plan: If minimum length is desired, with jack 6 ft (2 m) from ditch, step 16 yds (14 m) ('safe' ones) from rear ditch, and lay front of mat about nine inches to a foot (25-30 cm) less than the last yard. You will then not be caught in a challenge.

CORRECT GRIP

No phase of the game has called forth more diversity of opinion, hot air, and debate, than this question of gripping the bowl. As in most matters, the great majority, outside of

19

those who desire guidance, are swayed by the habits they have acquired, and argue along those lines.

It may be said that I do the same. True! But my arguments are backed up by 100 per cent achievement, the test of a lifetime and have been accepted as logical, conclusive, and sound.

Nature hadn't bowlers in view when she decreed small hands for the great majority of humans, and this is where the glove pinches. As mentioned elsewhere, the Australian Bowls Council foresaw this difficulty, and set out to overcome it by legislating for various sizes in bowls.

As that body knew that any sized bowl could be sat in the palm of the hand, making sizes and weights of no consideration, it is conclusive evidence that at least the majority had in mind the importance of finger and thumb manipulation in getting the best results.

Many players prefer to go for the weight in a bowl. Previously there was of necessity a relationship between the size and weight, the latter increasing with an increase in the major diameter. However, with improvements in the manufacture of composite bowls it has become possible to produce the same maximum weight irrespective of the size of a bowl, and the Australian Bowls Council and International Bowls Board have given their approval for the use of heavier bowls if so desired.

Many misguided friends of the beginner openly advocate the palm, or sitter, sometimes referred to as the claw.

It has been put forward that the proper way to hold a bowl is the comfortable way, but comfortable ways in lots of things in sport have been proved the wrong way.

You would not wear a glove or a boot much too big for you simply because of the comfort, but you would certainly combine comfort with correctness, and in bowls you can command that.

Anyhow, let us examine the subject: I will take the palmer first. He places his thumb at the side, either on or close to the disc. His finger-tips cannot be pressed close to the surface of the bowl, and he therefore loses the effect of that nerve sense that is essential to delicate touch. Players who palm the bowl are all more or less dumpers.

The thumb, being the most powerful member of the set, is

out of place at the side, and how is a player to give that life to the bowl which you impart to a billiard ball when you strike it correctly to put life into it, if there is no machinery such as the thumb provides for accomplishing it?

That being so, place the thumb anywhere on the running surface of the bowl, with the longest finger on the centre at the opposite side. It is not absolutely essential that the thumb should be in the centre; anywhere from the ring towards the centre, inwards, is just as effective. Personally, I find that for drawing purposes the nearer the centre the better.

Advice to roll the bowl gently off the tips of the fingers is a gay deceiver. Roll one off the tips, and it goes only a few feet, because it lacks the life-giving spin of the thumb. You can't roll and spin in one action.

The palm, claw, sitter devotee cannot ever put up a respectable case for the elimination of that powerful member of the hand that is the controlling factor in almost everything the hand is called upon to perform. We would be referred to as sissy if we attempted to throw a cricket ball in from the boundary without use of the thumb.

This advice is directed to those prepared to adopt it if convinced, not to a small section that being too long on the wrong track could not be brought back because they lack the will so to do.

The human hand presents us with four fingers and a super-finger. The first-named have three joints apiece, and the second two joints; the latter much the more powerful. The soft balls of the whole five, in the first joint, are the delicate feelers that just cover the nerve sense, and when these five agents contact the surface of a bowl they produce what we know as touch.

But place the bowl in the hand, as the sit-claw-palm artist must, which process misses the soft balls and delicacy of the nerve sense, just below their surfaces, and the delivery becomes more of a put than anything else.

Spin cannot be eliminated from bowling on any kind of green. It is the final, split-second agency that gets the required revolutions and life without effort out of and into the bowl. How can a player get spin or impart life into a bowl from the points or parts of the hand where it sits, apart from the fact that the nerve sense is not there?

That indispensable agent, the thumb, and its brothers, the fingers, are in entire sympathy in all things we handle, and you simply cannot separate them in bowls. In conjunction they give power, direction, produce that great essential, streamlined, and cause the bowl to do things that are positively lost to the palm-sitter.

Why do all (without exception) those whom I teach, or have taught, possess an accurate, rhythmical, powerful, and head-wrecking firm shot and drive? Ask any of them, and they will tell you that it is the grip of the bowl, as I propound it, and have used it to a success possibly unequalled by any one. 'You have a good hand,' someone will say. I reply, 'So have you if you will use the correct size bowl.' This contingency was foreseen by the A.B.C. Special Committee.

You know what 'centre of gravity' is, of course? Just look at the illustration (Fig. 2) and then grip your bowl with the thumb on the centre, long finger also on centre, with other fingers spread comfortably—not touching one another. Then hold the bowl up to the level of your head, and show the thumb underneath, as per Fig. 4.

Allow all the fingers to straighten out, and you have the bowl halved—centre of gravity. This means balance, which is one of the leading factors in bowls from several angles: If the palmer or claw gripper held his bowl up thus, it would fall sideways to the ground, because it lacks centre of gravity, or balance.

So that, in studying the relation of the bowl to the hand, you must take into consideration the necessity for a perfect fit. Many good thumbs can manage a bowl with 'weight', although displaying only short fingers, and judgment has to be shown there. By all means get the weight if possible, but don't sacrifice the correct grip to it (see Fig. 5).

The newcomer would be well advised to take a bowl home and keep it handy, and at every opportunity take hold of it and practise gripping or holding it correctly. That begets muscle moulding and setting, and it is surprising how the hand will conform to permanency with this practice.

We have now completed the second link in the Combina-

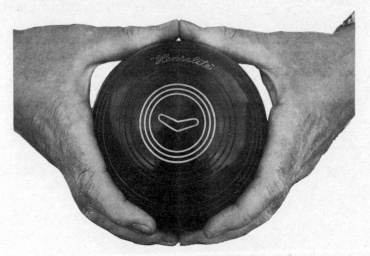

Fig. 1—The method of gripping the bowl as a guide to the correct size to use, as devised and advocated by the author. See page 17 for explanation.

Fig. 2—Demonstrating centre of gravity. Bowl balanced naturally on the ball of the thumb; when fingers are closed down is ready for delivery. The 'palmer' cannot accomplish this.

Fig. 4—Fingers should be 'streamlined', and not lie across the surface of the bowl. Longest finger must be exact centre.

Fig. 3—Thumb grip of R. T. Harrison. This bowl would be grassed on the backhand. For forehand play, half-way between centre and the first ring gives best results. Where there is slight strain, closer to rings is desirable.

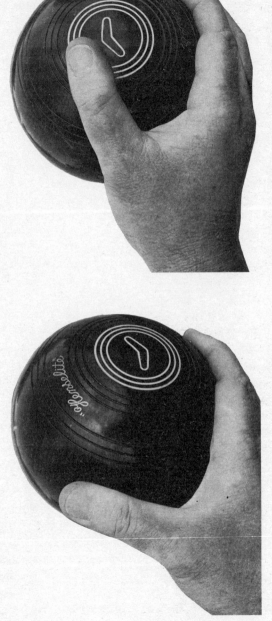

Fig. 5—Another view of the R. T. Harrison grip from a different angle. Disregard statements that the thumb is only a steadier.

Fig. 6—Grip of the 'palmer', necessitating sitting the bowl in the palm of the hand, with thumb at side, thus losing power of spin, nerve sense, and consequent loss of touch.

tion chain, by securing the bowl that suits or fits the hand, and learning how to grip it correctly. The student may meet with much opposition in the grip connection, but he will note that his advisers are mostly, if not invariably, palmers themselves. What he has to keep in mind is the fact that he must model his game on someone's, and the question then arises whether it is not prudent to discard old-time methods in favour of a modern one.

BALANCED STANCE IS MAINSPRING OF A BOWLER'S OUTFIT

STANCE, in relation to sport, is a preliminary or preparatory position that we place ourselves in so that we may be enabled to bring about a desired result. Balance is one of the most important factors in most games, and the close relation stance has to balance is obvious; but not in any game have men adopted so many modes of balancing themselves as in bowls. A boxing instructor sees to it early that his charge adopts an efficient method that will prevent him from being knocked off his feet easily, and the golfer, cricketer, billiardist, and others in a lesser degree also pay strict attention to this important subject. In bowling there are at least a dozen styles, or methods, which the newcomer does not necessarily choose, but has forced upon him. When left to himself he, being uneducated in the importance of correct balance, falls into one all his own, and it is mostly the wrong one.

Assuming, as we do, that we indulge in most games for the purpose of obtaining the maximum of exercise they afford, we naturally look for the best method of exercising all the muscles of the body, and not merely some of them. It is an accepted fact among experts that a body is physically healthier when any kind of exercise is spread over the whole of the anatomy, and, having this fact in view, we are enabled to approach the question of stance in bowls from an angle that is positively convincing.

Let us take what I will term some wrong or unbalanced stances as examples. We started off by approaching the game correctly; we got the bowl that we needed, and subsequently found how it should be held or gripped. Now, if we want to get a sweet, smooth delivery, we must be taught how to stand so that delivery will be natural and machine-like.

If one places the left foot out in front of him, standing erect, as many do, he will find that besides being unbalanced and easily pushed over from the side, the left leg muscles, from the ankle to the top of the thigh, are loose and flabby, while all the weight is being placed on the right leg.

Now take another of these so-called stances: A player places his left foot forward, his left hand on his knee, and balances his right leg and that side of his body on the front portion of his right foot—that is a very common method. Here again all the weight and work are borne by one side of the body—the left in this case. How many know that good balance begets good length?

Now a third: A player is often seen stooping and laying the bowl on the green, as seen in illustration (Fig. 7), then rising and delivering it. Here again one portion of the body is receiving more than its share of the burden, and balance is conspicuous by its absence. I might go through many other modes, and expose the same weakness, viz, certain muscles of the body getting all the strain, while others get little, and some none.

Obviously, then, any style that will exercise the whole of the body at once is not only the one we should adopt, but the one which should return us the maximum of good health. All this apart from what in reality the keen bowler is seeking uppermost—the stance which will give him the best results. After all, to keep all the muscles fit is contributing largely to that end in itself.

What mode or method, then, is there that will give us what we seek? I have written many times, and still submit, that there is only one stance for the bowler, and that is one that cannot fail to exercise every one of the muscles in the human body.

Now the method: After determining the position, walk on to the mat, place heels together, toes apart in military fashion, and bend the spine so that you will 'fall' naturally over your work, and the arms stretched out with the strain just sufficient to make them feel comfortable. The bowl should be held at a standard elevation, liable to change, according to length.

27

Fig. 7—Cramped, stooping 'stance', balance precarious, much to be avoided. Note that the player is laying the bowl on the green before delivering it.

Now, any medical man, if consulted, will tell you that with calves and thighs rigid, both shoulders employed exactly similarly, and the abdomen well tucked under, so that you comfortably feel the pressure under the belt, every muscle of the body is 'on guard,' from the top of the head to the very soles of the feet.

If you have had any experience in running, you will know that when the order to 'get set' comes, every muscle, and not merely some of them, has to be brought into requisition; but in nothing do all the muscles get so well and equally exercised as in the stance at bowls that I have consistently propounded.

It is not my province to condemn the methods of those who propound the 'stand upright' stance, but I think the true explanation why they still advocate that particular mode is because they began that way, and possibly think that it would be admitting too much to decry it now. While the 'upright' has everything on others—bar the one I teach— it has drawbacks that will finally appeal when the student reasons out the pros and cons.

The bolt-upright manner of standing leaves the abdominal muscles unexercised, and invites the fat to accumulate, the ultimate result later in life, if not early, being the dreaded 'corporation' and the discomforts arising therefrom—often reaching the heart. Also the muscles of the front of the thighs get insufficient work.

And from a purely bowling point of view, there is another fatal reason against a man standing erect. In every case he must hold his bowl up nearer to his chest, or shoulder, than when bending over his work with arms stretched out. Consequently, he has not the same command, and has actually to go through one more action, if not two, before he finally grasses the bowl.

Ask yourself whether a bowl grassed by a bending effort, or by an already bent one, would give greater control to the deliverer. It surely answers itself. Therefore, in the case of tall men, particularly, the nearer they get to the earth right away—they must get down sooner or later, and why not at once?—the better for their delivery, and also there is nothing to break in on their concentration.

In this lesson I am only emphasising correct stance, and no

29

mention of stepping, or delivery. We have now reached the stage when we are set for delivery, with the right approach to the game; the bowl that we need for our particular hand; the correct manner of holding it; and now the proper way to stand before delivering it. Thus, piece by piece, link by link, we become the perfect machine, and if we don't impatiently rush off to a green to try ourselves out, we will surely work into a human linotype at the finish, and produce results of a highly satisfactory nature.

Trying to get ahead of themselves ruins the future of many beginners. Delivery will be the next subject. Meantime, get the habit of having a bowl at home handy, so that you may homework yourself by gripping the bowl as taught, and now standing as required. You must not yet make any attempt at delivering, or stepping out—just holding the bowl with the correct grip and posing—many employ the mirror— with back bent and arms outstretched, the left hand simply supporting its side of the bowl.

DELIVERY—PRODUCT FROM GOOD OR BAD METHODS

GOOD or bad delivery at bowls is the natural outcome or consequence of a correct or incorrect approach to the game. Thus, if we succeed in getting the ideal bowl for the hand, and learn to hold it properly, then in holding it correctly also stand balanced, and use all our muscles in proportion, a good delivery is bound to follow. If, on the other hand, we adopt a bowl too large for comfort, necessitating going to the side with the thumb, and even stand correctly, our delivery suffers. We might get the right bowl, hold it as we should, but adopt a wrong or unbalanced stance, and again we fail to dovetail. The beginner will now see the reason for taking the combination of actions that make the perfect bowler, piece by piece, and stage by stage.

We have now arrived at the point when the learner must improvise a mat of his own, or obtain a regulation one of 24 in x 14 in (61 cm x 35.5 cm) and use it exclusively at home. Just as a projectile is shot out of a piece of artillery, and finds its mark by virtue of the mechanism, without which

Fig. 8—Correct stance. All muscles brought into action, and calculated to keep abdomen natural and normal. The bowl is held about 12 in (30.5 cm) below the face, and approximately 2 ft 6 in (76 cm) from the ground, but liable to be raised or lowered according to pace of green on the day. Note that the left foot faces the line to the kitty.

it would be useless, so the player must be armed with parts or supports sufficiently mechanical to cause his bowl to finish close to the kitty. If he has learned the preceding lessons correctly, he is so armed, and delivery becomes a gift as sweet and easy as driving a good car.

Having obtained the mat, just pick up a bowl and walk on to it without any attempt at anything. Stand approximately in the centre, and then place heels together, back naturally bent, and hold the bowl as instructed, with arms out in front, but not too rigid. The bowl for this lesson should be held approximately 2 ft 6 in (76 cm) from the ground, but with very tall men, say 3 ft (91.5 cm).

Now the learner should look himself over. He must do all the things he has been taught. He should say to himself, in effect: 'I have approached the game correctly (No 1); I have secured the bowl that suits my hand (No 2); I have learned to hold it as I should (No 3); I am standing balanced and comfortable (No 4); and now I must bring all these essentials into practice.'

Let us assume that we are actually about to send up a bowl so that it will finish right on kitty. What we sow at the mat end, that we must expect to reap at the jack end. So to proceed: There are two 'hands' at bowls—back and fore—and we will use the latter. Pick up the bowl, walk on to mat, place heels together with toes outward, bend over work, gripping as taught, and we are set for concentration. Left toe should point straight at kitty.

But we are early for concentration; all we must think about for the moment is that we are systematising our game with a view to an end, and following the Combination implicitly. So that when we are set, having no kitty in view, or not having to think about where we are going to roll the bowl, we begin to step out, just going through the motions of delivering without ever letting the bowl out of the hand.

Thus the student becomes moulded with much practice, doing nothing else for some time. This is the stage where great restraint must be maintained. I call it laying the foundation of the prospective champion's career, and if he desires to achieve success he must not look any further ahead for a while. I am now writing about the homework that is essential to every learner, and which applies equally to the man who is not too far gone.

As often as possible—a dozen times a day—pick up the bowl and just go through these motions, with short step, and always (at present) standing on the mat where I have indicated. Face fore and back hands at will; but just step shortly. Thus we are laying a solid foundation, and our muscles become set, or moulded, and give to us that sweet, balanced, rhythmical delivery as shown in Fig. 9.

After the bowl is brought right back for the delivery, the left foot should advance and the left hand drop from supporting the bowl naturally on to the knee. It is all one action—the poetry of motion. Many players step out first, and then bring the bowl back. That is fatal to balance, for all must work in unison. After some weeks, the mover gets confidence, and he can then take the longer steps; but for all purposes the shorter step is better for the moment. Don't practise firm shot or driving deliveries in these motions; have patience—they come of their own accord, and with the movements.

My sole object at this stage is to get the prospective champion to produce in himself and his action an exact facsimile of the illustration of the bowler shown in Fig. 9. When someone, or his mirror, can tell him that he has succeeded, he has laid a foundation that will stand for all time. Ending with delivery, this is the bowler's half-way house, where he must temporarily camp, and be prepared to make such a machine of himself that he can approach the next half of his education confidently feeling that he is ready.

Our next lesson will be on 'taking-green,' but the student should refrain from a study of this until he has become the moulded muscle-set, delivery-machine I have endeavoured to make him. Concentrate on that first half, make the foundation solid and lasting before approaching what will, in reality, be a test of intelligence, and the student's ability to pass examination. Swing, swing, and keep on swinging at home, even after entering the practical part of the next lessons. Be careful to face well outward, when going through the motions at home, on either hand; especially avoid bowling across the knees on the backhand—an early bad habit easy to acquire.

Fig. 9.—This photo shows simultaneous action of joints. Also eyes should be looking ahead, not down at the green.

DRAMA IN FOUR ACTS

PLACING the bowl on the kitty from the mat, on either hand, is a drama of the four following acts:—

1—PREPARATION (3-4 seconds interval)
2—POISE (3-4 seconds interval)
3—CONCENTRATION
4—JUDGMENT OF LENGTH

Preparation means getting the feel and bringing the nerves to the surface before poising. Poise means holding the bowl out in front of you. Concentration means taking in the necessary green width; and judgment of length speaks for itself. There should be a short interval between each.

TRAINING THE EYE IN VISIONING CORRECT GREEN

HAVING laid the foundation on which we build our future for better or worse, we come to the point where we must put the acid test upon the methods laid down in the first four links of the combination chain. We have the bowl most suitable to the hand, the method of gripping it to the greatest advantage, of standing so that we get the maximum of balance, power and control, and, lastly, the satisfactory delivery that comes to us from the system. I never fail to impress upon the newcomer, or early beginner, the importance of not being in a hurry to get past and leave behind this grounding work, ending with delivery. A colt is taught to carry gear, walk correctly, canter, and go through other ground work before being asked to gallop. He is built up with preliminary exercises, and moulded in just such another way as we build ourselves up in those first four grounding lessons. Therefore, don't be in a hurry to reach the 'galloping' stage.

When the student feels that he is working satisfactorily at home, gripping, standing, and stepping sweetly, placing his bowl on imaginary kitties, he can turn to the second half of his education and the serious business of becoming proficient in compiling points. In order to obtain them he has to employ, in a few seconds on the mat, all the parts of the machinery he has so carefully acquired. We now approach the fine points of the game.

The first lesson of this second series begins with how to determine the best method of getting close to that kitty, through the devious ways that come about by the constant alteration to the lie of the head. We use the term 'taking green' to indicate the track, or curve, that the bowl must take in order that it might lie just where we want it.

This lesson has mostly to do with judgment in taking the amount of green necessary, relative points, such as touch and length, coming with the next.

Walking on to the mat, take one look at the bowl, bend your back, and pose ready for concentration. That is the point at which you must fasten your gaze on the objective.

Making the correct curve to the kitty is brought about by concentration. When the player is set, he should not be in a hurry to 'go off.' Many go off half-cock, and almost invariably their bowls are too thin and roll towards the opposite boundary. Keep the eyes off the kitty, and take your line through the shoulder to the bank. It may be the next rink number, or some distinctive object.

The student will naturally find disappointment, because he will not have developed length, but that will come with practice, and will be dealt with in the next lesson. But wherever his bowl goes, or stops, in learning to 'take green' correctly, he must never forget one important consideration.

Although the whole business only takes a few seconds, he must do all the things he has been taught with the delivery of every bowl he sends up. He must not throw anything overboard, but grip the same, stand the same, and deliver the same. A train may go faster, but the same machinery is used to make it go slow or fast.

Don't favour one hand in your game. Always face well in the direction that the bowl is to go. If playing on the backhand, face slightly wider than the maximum point of your draw, and you will seldom be narrow. The same applies to the forehand, but as 75 per cent of men play narrow on the backhand through bowling across the knees, early care must be taken to form a habit of facing well away to the direction of that maximum point.

36

A previous edition advised beginners not to adopt spots and bank objects as guides to width of greens. I had been an accepted good billiardist, and knew angles at sight well. But teaching revealed that 95 per cent knew little or nothing of billiards, and angles, so I switched to bank objects, with startling results. Also improved my own game by the switch over. The latter gives an aiming line; the former doesn't. That aiming line is all-important, and minimises pinching.

WHY THOUSANDS OF NARROW BOWLS ARE PLAYED

HAVING satisfactorily, we assume, disposed of the question of proper and incorrect grips, or holds, let us turn to another subject that is vexed and contentious.

The great and final goal for all players is to be closer to that little white kitty than the opposition, through the devious ways peculiar to the game.

The choice of ways, then, becomes of paramount importance.

Fig. 10 shows a unique method of how to prevent pinching on either hand, otherwise running narrow, and so becoming useless, mostly. (Fig. 10 overleaf)

Possibly you have no conception of the hundreds of thousands of bowls played every week by those who stand wrongly on the mat, without due regard to correct facing, or going the direction they should go.

Fig. 10 demonstrates the top half of a clock. At 12 there is a kitty placed on the centre of the rink. Now look at the figure playing the forehand. Note that the left foot points straight at 12 o'clock, or kitty, and the right straight at 3 o'clock.

A second picture would demonstrate the reverse, or backhand. The right foot points at 12 of the clock, and the left at 9 o'clock. In each instance this stance, causing the body to face in the required direction, prevents narrow bowling —the bugbear of all.

Take up a bowl and work it out. Lay the mat and place a jack at any distance. As you walk on to the mat, the intention being to draw on the backhand, the right foot automatically and naturally points to the kitty.

Fig. 10—Demonstrating correct 'facing' and position of feet when drawing. Playing on the forehand the left foot is facing to 12 o'clock, while the right foot points approximately to 3 o'clock. Reverse for the backhand.

Bringing the left foot, military action, up so that heels are together, toes out, you become set, and should very seldom play narrow. You will do so occasionally, despite everything, but the percentage will be small.

It will also improve your balance, your curve imagination, and your length and game generally. Many players go to a facing extreme, resulting in round-arming their bowls, and this is fatal.

The exact angle is there, and should be made. It is easy and simple. Your whole body, shoulders, knees, hips, eyes, should face the direction the bowl must take.

Note, then, how the other items dovetail: If you follow the teachings, you hold your bowl so that the rings, the running surface consequently, the fingers of your hand, and the thumb all face the one way.

Isn't that logical and practical? If you have failed in these things, and now adopt them, you will assuredly find that your anatomy will respond; you will be better physically, and your game improve immensely.

Always provided, of course, that you carry out the contract to bend over your work, avoiding any semblance of the erect —standing quite upright—method.

HOW LENGTH AND TOUCH MAY BE ACQUIRED

LENGTH, touch, control of the bowl come with practice; like nursery cannons at billiards, they have to be acquired. To secure these essentials a foundation or grounding has to be carefully prepared, and as we have succeeded in that direction, we are now ready to observe whether or not we have a natural bent for that delicate manipulation necessary in controlling the bowl on a fast green (16-18 sec) and placing it about the kitty. Many men, highly strung ones in particular—golfers, good cueists, ex-cricketers, and others used to ball games— make good very quickly at bowls, as a rule, while others are absolutely void of all ideals of touch and manipulation. While the former come to hand and show up inside two or three seasons, the latter take considerably longer to develop, and with these we are mostly concerned. The ranks of bowlers

DITCH

CUTTING THE GREEN
UP INTO 3 LENGTHS   ◯   Jack, 108 ft (33 m)

                         ◯   Jack, 87 ft (26.5 m)

                         ◯   Jack, 66 ft (20 m)

Minimum length | MAT | 16 yds (15 m) from
66 ft (20 m)   rear ditch

Medium length | MAT | 9 yds (8 m) from
87 ft (26.5 m)   rear ditch

Full length | MAT | 2 yds (1.8 m) from
108 ft (33 m)   rear ditch

Keep in your bowling mind the figures shown on diagram, and they will soon become automatically set there, enabling you to judge a length at sight.

contain a fairly big army of men who never indulged in any kind of sport or outdoor game, and they are the most difficult to teach.

But for all purposes, and irrespective of persons, there are means that will give length and touch, and we will proceed right away in an attempt to develop them. We will have to go back, temporarily, however, to that portion or stage in our education where we were taught to clasp the bowl with fingers and thumb, so that the ball or nerve-points are given full scope.

The reason for condemning the palm, sitter, or claw grips will now be evident, as will the reason for propounding the grip that compels the player to feel, through the ball of his fingers and thumb, that nerve sense which is the very essence of touch and strength. The palmer loses the benefit of nerve sense.

The student does not require to go out and play to a kitty with the object of getting on or close to it, but should solely concentrate on length for quite a good while. The urge to get into a game will be great, but it should be curbed. Keep out of competitive games until the education is completed.

Therefore, take the line of the four, six, or eight bowls used in length practice, rather than their distance from the white. A student will get on the kitty soon enough after learning to control his length. It must never be forgotten— and cannot too often be remembered—that the systematising which we have been taught is the principal agent in acquiring what we now seek.

We walk on to the mat with the correct bowl to suit our hand; we know how to grip or hold it; we also know how to stand correctly; and these are followed with a naturally good delivery. Having conquered the art of 'taking green' as per our last lesson, everything dovetails in so sweetly that there is no reason now why we should not begin to show the results of our labours.

Let us take an actual example: We take out four, six, or eight bowls, with the object of spending an hour by ourselves —no mates—to master length. Place a kitty first of all 75 ft (23 m) up the green. Now we walk on to the mat, and in the

41

half-dozen seconds necessary to do all the things we have been taught send up the first bowl.

Play all forehand for a quarter of an hour, and all backhand for the next quarter, alternately. Say our first bowl runs 10 ft (3 m) beyond the kitty, demonstrating that the effort is too strong; we immediately ask ourselves the cause. The system cannot be blamed; it is something that puzzles us.

I have not up to now referred to a particularly important point, and which may be the cause of that bad bowl being 10 ft (3 m) strong. Jerking has no place in a good player's outfit; he must not show even the semblance of a jerk, for the slightest will cause a bowl to run too fast, giving that many extra revolutions not actually meant.

If the cause was not a jerk—ever so slight—what was it? Want of control, to be sure. Let us try another. Standing right, facing right, delivering with a jerkless effort; surely this time we must get on the line of length. We can get length without necessarily getting on kitty, and that is what we are after for the time being.

But we are again strong, and still puzzled. If the green is fast, or moderately so (13-14 sec), we may be taking too long a step, which, overbalancing us, causes the bowl to run stronger than we meant it to. The third one is better, 3 ft (1 m) beyond the line of kitty. A player may find that he has been holding the bowl too high up from the ground, losing control; and it is always wise to drop the bowl lower after a too-strong effort, for the weight of the article itself plays an important part in length.

By the time we have played eight bowls on that forehand, we begin to realise the great value of system, of doing everything we have learned; but in this length practice we must keep another important point in view continuously. It is what I term doing the same thing with every bowl.

At the end of the first half hour we begin to show some result of our labours, and getting much closer to the line—or imaginary line—of kitty; but many of our bowls are far from being good length. Many days' practice helps us, but there is still room for improvement.

There is an outstanding reason why, even with the best players in the big events, bad length is noticeable. We will leave the student and his lesson for a moment, and watch one

of the old-timers in a championship. He places his first bowl
9 in (23 cm) beyond the jack, and his second is 5 ft (1.5 m)
beyond.

His third is 2 ft (61 cm) short, although a good bowl, and
his fourth is 4 ft (1.2 m) short. Now that is a fair head, but
not good length. Why? Well, with his first he grassed his bowl
very sweetly, without any sign of jerk. If he had repeated the
effort, his second would have been with the first, but he did
something different—just a slight overstep, the merest jerk—
and he finished 5 ft (1.5 m) beyond the head.

Then, with the third bowl, he came back 7 ft (2.1 m) to be
2 ft (61 cm) off kitty, and with his fourth another 2 ft (61 cm)
shorter. We noticed that his last bowl had a bit of a wobble
on, and that was the cause of making him short, the same
strength being there, but not the even-keel motion that would
have got him on kitty. In teaching, one only deals with running greens (12-15 sec).

So the reason for doing the same thing with every bowl is
apparent. If the player sends one up with no wobble visible,
the next with a 'dump' and absence of final spin, a third with
a decided wobble, and the fourth differently delivered from
the other three, he will reap four different results in length.
What we sow at the mat end we reap at the jack end, let
me repeat.

If, on the other hand, we send up four bowls all the same,
sweetly and truly delivered, with no jerk, we get our reward
at the jack end with four similar bowls.

There is no hope for the man who does four different things
—he is all over the green—and he never becomes that heart-
breaking machine that is the despair of the opponent. A
player devoid of control of length seldom gets anywhere.

After half an hour on the forehand, take the backhand,
following the same set of rules. Note your line—If you have
one 4 ft (1.2 m) strong, one 4 ft (1.2 m) short, that is bad
length. Don't practise 75 ft (23 m) the next time; make it 100
ft (30.5 m) and the third day make it 66 ft (20 m).

After as much as he can get by himself at this, the student
should have an hour at the following, playing half an hour—
or whatever he likes—on each hand: Place a jack 66 ft (20 m)
up the green, another 87 ft (26.5 m) and a third 108 ft (33 m).

Take out eight bowls—the size specified, not bowls too big or too small—and play one at the 66 ft (20 m) jack, the next at the 87 ft (26.5 m) and the third at the 108 ft (33 m). Keep practising in this manner, taking the short or longer step for the short or longer lengths. With the experience gained in this lesson, the beginner will surprise himself—good for the old player, too.

Most followers of the game know nothing of the term 'bowling blind,' in relation to discovering the natural—or otherwise—aptitude for good length.

One prefers to keep the reader guessing rather than attempt to add to his perplexities by a recital of the details of this test. Suffice to add that it is very searching, and reveals one way or the other what is being searched for.

PRESENTING THE WILL TO WIN

THE will to win is a state of mind, a desire to excel, to get out of the ruck. I am referring to the not-so-good rank and filers, of course. The expression, 'mind over matter,' is often employed to indicate, or urge to greater effort, so that we may overcome any obstacle, if we possess a mind to do so. Without ability to back up will to win, or assumptions that mind can defeat matter, in bowls these sentiments have no value whatever.

Might as well attempt to make wine without grape-juice; lard out of mutton fat or beef dripping, as to accomplish the shots in the game necessary to succeed, merely through the will to win, however strong.

Confidence is a thing apart; without it nobody gets very far, for the combination of efficiency, confidence, and the strong will to win, is a treble that is mostly past the post before the race begins.

Every bowl has its value, and slow beginners often fall by the wayside through visualising defeat before it is imminent.

YOUR SINEWS—KEEP THEM ELASTIC

To be consistent, you must maintain muscular development and keep your sinews well stretched and elastic. Which means that when in the act of delivery the knee must be only inches from the ground.

When you fail to get down, it is an incentive to the sinews to drive you further up, until you eventually become a 'pitcher' or thrower.

Men come into the game, say at 40, and follow the bending of the knee process correctly for some years. Many have periods away from the greens, and the day after resuming develop soreness.

The next day sees them failing to get down on that account, and, with the years, they come still further up and up, until they are replicas of the model in Fig. 11.

THEORY OF ELEVATION

THEORY of Elevation in Bowls originated entirely with the author, and had never previously ever been approached in any treatise or work or by any individual. In fact, even now it is very little understood.

On the principle that a player should allow the weight of the bowl to get it on the kitty, increasing the elevation or lowering it according to length, this scientific method of breaking the hearts of opponents has been practised successfully for many years by myself.

We all know that if a bowl is placed on the chute of a testing table at a given point, it will roll to the exact spot every time. Make the run further, or elevate the bowl, and it will run a specified distance further. Give it a shorter run, or lower elevation, on the chute, and a lesser distance is traversed, but wherever placed the utmost accuracy is obtained.

On the principle that the human arm should be trained, in conjunction with the brain, and the 'do the same thing always' lesson, taught earlier in this treatise, to imitate the machine even approximately, the player becomes very mechanical. Like all the other subjects handled, this one is, of course, subject to correct or proper playing conditions.

To work the Elevation Theory correctly, the player must subject himself strictly to, and conform to, the lessons in their entirety, making himself a machine in grip, stance, delivery, and always bending the spine at a regular curve, or angle, so that his natural elevation is the same, were he measured from ground to chin at any time.

Fig. 11—With maturer years the player who had previously got close down to the green with his delivery finds himself 'coming up', owing to allowing the sinews to contract. As demonstrated in this picture, he becomes a dumper, pitcher, tosser of the bowl. His whole game deteriorates, spin and touch vanish, and the surface of the green suffers.

Elevation Theory demands that there be no jerking, and the length of step, according to state of green, has to be studied. Not many players succeed in conquering the intricacies of this department of the game, but those who do become the despair of their opponents, particularly in singles.

Points must be taken from the front of the mat. For instance, if you stand on the centre of the mat and send up your first bowl, and it drops 6 ft (2 m) short, you know at once that there is not sufficient weight behind the effort. Therefore, you raise the bowl slightly, which gives the added weight, and you make that shortage up.

With the Elevation Theory the elementary lessons come to an end. That does not mean, however, that there is no more to be said or learned concerning them. In the later pages each of the eight points that make up the Combination are dealt with from different angles. The reason for separating the elementary from the more advanced teaching will be understood after perusal of the latter. It would, indeed, be a mistake to load the student with the intensely finer points until his fundamenal education is complete.

SWING AND STEP RHYTHM

FOR firm shots and drives, standardise the elevation or height from the green that is necessary to produce a split-second timed delivery.

This must be determined according to the inches of the player. A tall man would require to hold his bowl higher from the sward than a short man, of necessity.

Such standardisation would have this effect: The firm shot, or drive, would be grassed with a rhythm that makes direction and control just what these terms stand for.

Further, the player's muscles and sinews become permanently set by this process, and jar is entirely eliminated. It is not brute force that provides the speed, but what we know as knack.

The player who puts his bowl down sweetly is he who employs an approximate height when making fast shots.

It is different for the draw. Height in proportion to length of throw, and step taken, must be closely studied. A 5 ft 9 in

47

man (1.6 m) would step about 4 ft (1.2 m) and his swing would be not less than 9 ft (3 m) from rear to grassing point, when putting the pace on.

With the standard mat only 2 ft (61 cm) long and the law requiring the back of your heels to be inside the back edge of the mat. the maximum possible variation for the position of the feet is only 12 in (30.5 cm). Therefore, the adjustment of the pendulum swing of the arm has to be done entirely by judging the length of the forward step. This is indicated on page 41.

Assume that you are playing to a minimum (66 ft or 20 m) jack, you would stand approximately in the centre of the mat and with a short swing and a short step, let the weight do it to take it to the jack.

By simply raising the elevation, as shown for 87 ft or 26.5 m (medium) length, and taking a slightly longer step, the additional longer natural swing would propel the bowl the extra distance required.

Likewise, for the maximum length of 108 ft (33 m), a still higher elevation and again longer step will achieve the objective, and provided there is no jerk, how can you fail to make a machine of yourself?

Always providing, of course, that you take correct green and eliminate all suggestions of jerking.

SHORT ENDS WHEN GREENS ARE FAST

SHORT ends on extremely fast or fiery (18-20 sec) greens catch 95 per cent of players. One-length or constant-length steppers, are the human flies that easily become entangled in the 'short-end' web.

And yet any player can become really expert on these short ends. It is all a question of step, elevation, plus fingers, thumb, and wrist. Touch, thus acquired, enables the exponents to play the longer ends with more control also.

Fig. 12 clearly indicates the three positions of the body for the various lengths required. The first photograph gives the elevation at the extreme lowest—from your eye through the centre of the bowl to the point on the green where you intend to step.

Fig. 12—1.—When the surface is keen (16-18 sec.) the player should take his position as shown here for very short lengths, calling for a step of less than a foot. Note the low elevation of the bowl.

2.—For medium lengths the player should make the step slightly longer, in proportion to the longer swing and higher elevation.

3.—With a full length throw of the jack, the player raises his bowl elevation, and of course, extends his stride in order to maintain balance.

Peg   Rink No 4   Peg

Playing to
figures

108 ft (33 m)

Add 7 yards (7 m)

87 ft (26.5 m)

Add 7 yards (7 m)

66 ft (20 m)

Elevation for   108 ft (33 m) length

Elevation for   87 ft (26.5 m) length

Elevation for   66 ft (20 m) length

MAT

Only the slightest swing—about 12 inches (30.5 cm) back to your knees—is required, plus that life-giving thing we call a 'flick,' which in reality is spin, is needed to place your bowl round the kitty.

Here again we are forced to regard the possibility of the other fellow being just as expert as we may be in this department. In such a contingency the following firm and fast shot lessons supply the answer.

FIRM SHOT INTRICACIES AND HOW TO OVERCOME THEM

IN approaching the firm shot department of the game we have to assume that the student is ready to tackle that advanced stage in his education. Although we have to take the lessons as they come in sequence, as a matter of necessity, there is no reason why any half-learned one should be dropped in order to study what are, in reality, the finer points in the game that come with the constant application to the lessons ending with delivery. Just study that very carefully.

Become absolutely proficient in grip, stance, and delivery; get 'set' so that a flaw cannot be detected in your education up to the half-way house, and the rest will surely come. The student, though anxious to get along and keep pace with the latter instruction, should never tire of taking up that bowl at home, holding it as instructed, standing with a permanent natural curve of the spine—bending well over the job— arms extended, and finally short and long stepping out, without ever dropping the bowl. He can never get too much of it, employing both hands.

And now for the firm shot department: What is a firm shot, to begin with? Reason it out this way: We take up our position on the mat, and following out our system do all the things we have been taught, whatever shot is required according to the lie of the head.

The lie calls for a dead draw shot, but later in the game we are asked to be a little firm without losing the bowl. Naturally that means a little stronger and a little firmer than the draw, so we take less green, and slightly more pace, and increase our step.

51

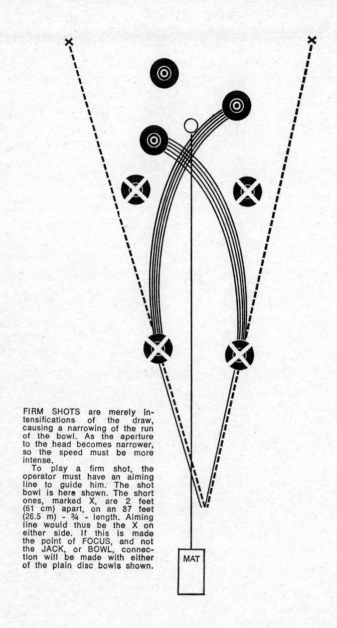

FIRM SHOTS are merely intensifications of the draw, causing a narrowing of the run of the bowl. As the aperture to the head becomes narrower, so the speed must be more intense.

To play a firm shot, the operator must have an aiming line to guide him. The shot bowl is here shown. The short ones, marked X, are 2 feet (61 cm) apart, on an 87 feet (26.5 m) - ¾ - length. Aiming line would thus be the X on either side. If this is made the point of FOCUS, and not the JACK, or BOWL, connection will be made with either of the plain disc bowls shown.

MAT

But understand this thoroughly: We don't depart from our methods; we grip the same, stand the same, and deliver the same, and therefore we can now answer the question. 'What is a firm shot?' by replying that it is simply an intensification of the draw. All firm shots, up to the fastest drive, are purely intensification of the draw, employing the same set of lessons in the use of each.

Firm shots consist of two different species. There is the first, consisting of little more than a draw, when the bowl would finish approximately 20 or 30 ft (6 or 10 m) beyond the head; the second, which on a running surface would necessitate about three feet of green on a minimum legth. There the firm shot series stop—anything faster would be a drive, and driving is a separate lesson.

I have taken much pains in instructing the student not to throw overboard any of his parts in the machine which, up to now, he has made of himself; he must not, and need not, worry about results at the other end if he does all the things taught him—they will work themselves out.

It has been demonstrated that for a draw, say, 100 ft (30 m) length on a normally running surface (12-14 sec), a step of two or three feet (60-90 cm) is sufficient to maintain balance. Therefore, if more weight and a slightly firmer effort are required, the step would increase.

Then, if a still firmer effort is required, the step must increase accordingly, all the time maintaining natural balance and control of the body and the bowl. So that by the time the maximum in firm shots is reached, we find that we have increased our step from 2 ft (60 cm) for the draw to at least 3 ft 6 in (1 m 15 cm). Again I emphasise: we must keep an ever-watchful eye on our system.

No jerking, no over-reaching, no different manner of standing, but a perfect rhythmical intensification of the simple draw shot when firming through. Many players tie themselves in all sorts of knots when asked to come through a head, or to play a fast, swinging shot. The only difference between a quiet dead-draw shot and a maximum firm one is that the effort is stronger in the latter case.

Of course, there is no fixed scale. On a fiery green (18-20 sec) a very short step, 9 in (23 cm) is all that is required for

53

the draw on minimum length. And in proportion for longer. And so for the firmer shots on such a surface the step should be in accordance—it is fatal to direction to over-reach.

But we may find ourselves on a heavy green (9-10 sec) which we often do, and then the step must be longer, both for the draw and the firm shots. It is all a question of maintaining correct balance, which as time goes on becomes second nature to the student. Care should be taken not to develop a jerk in that final flick from the fingers and thumb, for jerking cannot be regulated.

Getting up, after being short, is best regulated by raising the bowl that little bit higher, causing the weight to overcome the discrepancy, rather than by the common and bad habit of jerking it away. In 95 per cent of cases the jerk thus applied ends in the bowl running many feet beyond the head.

Good practice at home, on the lawn, or elsewhere, is to give your imagination play by standing on the mat and conceiving in the mind's eye a kitty 100 ft (30.5 m)—or any distance—away, and going through the motions—stepping out and 'taking green' as taught. No need to drop the bowl, the idea being to develop a permanent, jerkless swing, under all conditions and circumstances, also having regard to timing.

DRIVING—IN REASON

DRIVING in bowls is a very necessary part of the equipment of a first-class player. Without efficiency in this department none are first class. For the beginner, however, and those in the slightly more advanced stage, my counsel is to leave driving entirely alone until many weeks or months of drawing and firmer shot practice fit them for the very fast ones. Driving has been described as the refuge of a coward, but as with grip and stance, those sentiments come only from people who preach, not what should be done, but what they do. Bowls without driving would be a very drab sort of a pastime, and would very quickly develop into a game purely for the weak and ailing, both from a physical as well as a mental angle.

The student must reach the driving stage in his education sooner or later, but should not skip over the fundamentals, and undo the good work of gradual process by attempting the very strong shots until he feels that they come to him naturally.

54

If he moulds himself as laid down, firm shots to fast drives will produce themselves; he will not find it necessary to attempt to acquire them.

There has ever been a diversity of opinion on the question of what constitutes the most effective method of driving. The great majority favour what is, in reality, a firm shot, rather than a very fast, straight one. I have very pronounced opinions on this particular aspect.

Again, the majority favour and propound the firm shot rather than the fast one because they are quite unable to accomplish the latter. Many of our best lack the ability to drive a bowl absolutely straight, which leaves them that much short in efficiency, and consequently they run many seconds.

What constitutes the most effective method of driving? The query is somewhat ambiguous. It depends upon what shot is called for when deciding which variety should be used; therefore a player should have every variety of drive in his locker, not merely the bending one.

The oft-repeated argument that firm shots are more effective than the drives falls to the ground when someone is called upon to take all the bias off the bowl with a swift effort, and hasn't that shot in his locker. The firm shot player must get 'wrecked' in many of the lies on the green, even though a bowl or a kitty can be plainly seen on the head, and quite within the range of the fast driver to deal with.

Therefore, it is logical to assume that if a player hasn't got that fast, straight one, he is handicapped and loses many points in consequence. How many points that handicap constitutes in a match of 21 or 31 up is a matter of conjecture, but who can afford to give away points when arrayed against the best talent?

So, having settled the point, we shall proceed to the actual lesson in driving. The student has been taught that if he does all the things set out in separate lessons, he must become machine-like, and when he makes a fast or firm effort that machine-like action will assert itself.

There can be no doubt on that point. He finds himself balanced, and in driving balance plays a big and important part. Notice the Celestial with two heavy baskets attached to a pole, which he balances across his shoulders. Weight is equalised on both sides, and that allows him to walk quite comfortably while carrying his load.

That aspect comes in when driving. The player must stand on the mat with heels together, distributing the weight equally on both legs, and bringing every muscle in the body into play. The bowl should be held higher for the drive than for the draw, and the stance slightly more erect.

Balance must be maintained at all costs, and the faster the drive the longer the stride. The student should hold the bowl the same as taught in the draw, stand the same, and deliver the same, so that in driving his effort becomes an intensification of the draw, as previously explained. And, as with the draw, it should be a poetry of motion.

Why the bowl must come back to the fullest extent is because the long stride demands balance for the rest of the body—a long stride, a long drop back to the rear with the right arm, and a long swing forward, going with the effort in order to maintain equilibrium and absence of jerking. We term it the 'follow through,' because we go with the effort.

One of the fatal errors in driving is to sacrifice direction to speed. We need to keep control and get a better and more accurate line by driving slightly under our natural strength of limb. There is a limitless army of drivers who only hit occasionally, and they belong to that category. The accurate, straight drivers in most centres can be counted on the fingers of one hand.

The bowl should be held the same as for the draw, loosely at first, but tightening at the point of release. One of the common faults with players is dumping, or throwing the bowl down in front of them, instead of spinning it from the fingers and thumb. Many throw it a yard and further out in front of them; a lifeless thing that shows its 'eyes' as if in protest.

It is good practice to take a bowl home, swing it as often as possible with the long step motion, without letting it out of the hand, following through, either on carpet or lawn. Get into the exaggerated draw habit, the only difference being that of speed, slow dead-draw stuff, medium firm shot stuff, and then fast, and still faster. This moulding practice is excellent.

In getting direction we have to imagine that there is a

straight white line from the mat to the kitty, and bring the bowl back, not with a loop, but along that imaginary line and then straight back along it again, both efforts being approximately three to four inches past the right knee. Never 'loop' in driving—it is fatal to direction.

And now for one final hint in this department of the game. The great majority of men, after they reach fifty years of age, jerk their drives. They don't follow through, or let themselves go with the effort, because they have never set their muscles as does an athlete practising getting out of his holes for sprinting.

The older men get the more cramped becomes their action, unless they have early learned the art of going with the effort. We see the average driver keep his right leg behind the left at the moment of delivery, jerking the bowl away, as if afraid that something might snap if he let himself go.

Therefore, develop the 'trot through': I often finish yards up the green as a consequence of going with a very fast one and maintaining my balance. See Fig. 15. Increasing years will not call for a halt in that direction, as to follow through is all part of the rhythmic and machine-like delivery which comes from placing the heels together and allotting each limb its quota.

Timing the drive, with treble-swinging action, is a product of, and often used by, myself, and an act only acquired by practice. Without correct timing—releasing the bowl to a split second—consistent direction is not obtained. See Fig. 13 for this movement.

I have been queried at different periods: 'Why the to-and-fro swing?' Ask a billiards expert why he moves the cue to-and-fro over the bridge formed by the hand on the table.

Ask the baseball pitcher why he finds it necessary to make several movements of the body before he delivers the ball; the putter at golf why he makes preliminary movements with the club.

All come under the same category. Stand on the mat with heels together, elevate the bowl about the height of the hips with both hands, then swing both arms back approximately the same distance behind you. Single, slow-motion action also makes for good driving.

Fig. 13—Grassing the bowl for a well-timed fast drive. First movement began when the feet were together on the mat. Within a split second the driver's right hand would be up level with his face, and his body following through. For the purpose of instruction the player here has deliberately stepped too far with the left foot. See next page for correction. Avoid advice to step only as you would if walking for all lengths. Study the proved raising and lowering method in Fig. 12.

Fig. 14—A clean follow-through, after a fast drive, conforming to balance and swing.

Fig. 15—Following through after a very fast effort. The mat is at the rear of the player.

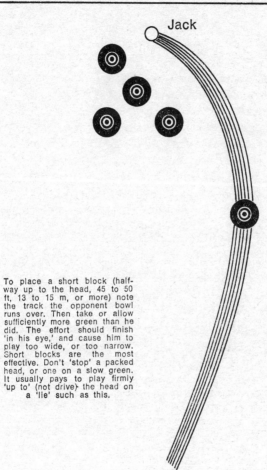

3   4   5

Jack

To place a short block (half-way up to the head, 45 to 50 ft, 13 to 15 m, or more) note the track the opponent bowl runs over. Then take or allow sufficiently more green than he did. The effort should finish 'in his eye,' and cause him to play too wide, or too narrow. Short blocks are the most effective. Don't 'stop' a packed head, or one on a slow green. It usually pays to play firmly 'up to' (not drive) the head on a 'lie' such as this.

MAT

ACCURATE BLOCKING BRINGS MANY POINTS

BLOCKING is not generally practised, firstly because a great many consider its value negligible, and secondly because most bowlers lack what is known as the 'angle' eye. There is another reason, which can best be dealt with as we go along.

Why is the 'block' necessary in the game of bowls? By answering that question I will also answer those who think it is not essential, and often refer to a bowl played short as 'a waste of a good wood.' When a man builds himself a nice comfortable residence and lays out a garden in keeping, he does not leave it thus, but proceeds to erect a fence round the whole.

If he did not, he would leave his property open to all-comers, but by taking this precaution, he protects himself from encroachments. In other words, fitting to our subject, what is the use of erecting a house unless you protect it as suggested? Apply this to your game.

What is the use of building up a head, lying any number of shots, or even if it be only a single, if the path is left open to the opposition to get in and beat you to it? Mostly the reason why many skips fail and do not actually drop one 'in his eye' is that they either choose the wrong place on the green or play too narrow.

Assume that we are lying shots and desire to 'shut the gate' in an attempt to hold them. We first have to decide a very important point, and that is as to the lie of the head, and great judgment has to be shown in this connection.

If the green is keen, or reasonably fast-running (15-17 sec), and the bowls are not too clustered, the block shot is very desirable, but if the lie is 'big,' and the green is not 'taking' too widely, it is fatal to block, as 95 per cent of skips will immediately 'play into' the group, and all the good work goes up in smoke, and, instead of them being in trouble, we find ourselves there instead.

Also, judgment should be shown in knowing your man in the blocking business. Some men immediately get to work with the drive as soon as a head become congested, while

62

many others will continue to draw until they get first or second shot. It is with the latter that a risk can be taken.

There are many very good players, in both the singles and fours connection, that the block is fatal to. It gets their morale and looms large in their vision. That is where we must exercise our judgment in selecting cases for the block shot.

Never make the mistake of blocking for a single, where the shot bowl can be seen, or can be got at, for when they take that shot out it often leaves them in possession, sometimes of several, and puts you where you would have them.

Now as to values. I have said previously that the short block makes for the best obstruction. Undoubtedly it does. If approximately placed only, it compels most opponents to keep shy, and causes them to take either too little green, running narrow, or too much, running wide.

The latter aspect applies particularly to straight bowls that fail to make or come in when the green is not drawing much. But what we want to get at is the art or ability to place a block half-way up the green, known as a short one.

I have frequently called for a shot of this description with a third man's last bowl, but with mostly the same experience. Almost all play it as though they were bowling right up to the head. Let me give an example:

Assume that we have a 100-ft (30.48 m) length. A player would take certain green to get on to the jack, and does so. Then he is asked by his skip to drop in a short block—half-way up. Angle-blind some bowlers are, and the man who takes the same country for blocks half-way up the green is in this category.

We have to see a jack on the exact line, half-way up, that was taken to get the first on the white, and 'take green' sufficiently to place the bowl there. If we take the same amount for the short block effort as for a long-drawn shot we run narrow—from a yard to several more feet, according to the pace of the surface.

In short, always use more green—according to judgment—for a short block effort than for a long-draw shot. Think that out, and also work it out on a piece of paper with your pencil. On fiery greens (19-21 sec) it is surprising how many more feet you must use with a short block in view, because the bowl begins to 'work' almost at once.

For three-quarter blocks the same principle is followed, but this species has to be very perfect to be effective. With the long block (that one that urges the average skip to try to get round) great precision is necessary. In the majority of cases skips endeavouring to place a long block run narrow, for very few take the necessary amount of country.

After all, the art of blocking lies in the eye. First pick the exact spot where the bowl must drop or the line it is assumed the opponent must run over, and then forget that there is anything else on the green. All other bowls and objects can be got out of the vision if blockers concentrate on that given spot. Have we not frequently heard a skip call: 'Don't look at that short bowl; it is not in your way a bit.'

To know when to block and to know when to leave it alone, like driving, must be left to the player, but one thing I will repeat and emphasise: Never block a big head, for even the most mediocre opponent has some kind of a firm shot, and many bowlers are gamblers and will give it a fly, with the sentiment always present that 'you never know your luck.'

SCIENCE OF DEFEATING THE BLOCK

FEW bowlers, even advanced ones, realise the assistance that can be obtained by the intelligent application of being allowed to stand on the mat adjacent to either side and to step off it in any forward direction. It is also something too deep for the average propagandist.

This forward and/or side-stepping ability will be best understood by an examination of Figs. 16, 17, 18 and 19. These will explain the various phases propounded in this subject matter, and as each is taken separately the reader should examine the particular illustration dealing with that angle.

The mat is in reality only a base from which our operations must be carried out. It also has another use in that it protects the green, but to the competitive player it is essentially only a base for determining the position of one foot at the moment of delivery.

During the course of a game the average player would stand

in the centre, either a little nearer the front or nearer the back, for ordinary draw work, but when he finds that he is blocked on the route by short, narrow bowls, and has to get round or inside one of these to reach the head, he must use his brains and calculating power, so that he does not become 'wrecked' on the way.

I have taught in the earlier lessons that 'what we sow at the mat end we reap at the jack end,' and that slogan is a good one for all departments of the game. In an attempt to avoid going on the rocks, or getting past an obstructing short bowl, or bowls, we have to do something that is different from the normal draw, so that the bowl will run up the green along a different line, thereby avoiding a collision.

Let us assume, as a first lesson in this subject, that the opposition has planted a bowl half-way up the green and right on the track, or 'in his eye,' as we understand the term. This block has often a very demoralising effect on the cautious, which I will refer to when dealing with this subject of blocks generally.

What must we do to get either round or inside a bowl half-way up the green and right in our track? Numerous points may be lying against us, and we must pass it and be up at all costs. The first thing a player must decide in such a case is not to allow the lie to get his morale—to many that obstruction becomes as big as a football, because they keep looking at it.

Now look at Fig. 16. It is using the mat so as to be able to get inside the block. It would not be any use merely to get inside without reaching the head in such a manner that the player's bowl would finish close to kitty, either to 'save' or to get the actual shot. It is quite simple to get inside or outside of any block with a narrow or wide effort, but neither of these would finish within the territory necessary.

Note the position of the feet on the mat. They are so placed that on grassing the bowl it is put down considerably narrower than a normal draw, and yet takes, 'virgin country' up to the obstructing bowl point. Such a grassed bowl does not begin its bending work until within six feet of the block, whereas with a normal draw the work begins many yards sooner.

65

That fact—that the bowl sent up along virgin country does not begin to bend until close to the obstruction—makes it certain that the maximum draw of the bowl will be delayed until nearing the head, and it will assert itself and come in as though no block had existed.

Imagine that there is a similar block on the forehand—the previous one being on the forehand also—and we desire to get round it. Note the position of the feet on the mat in Fig. 17. By grassing the bowl nine inches to a foot on the extreme right of the mat, at a point nearest to the rear, we sow in virgin soil, and the draw, although normal, takes us on to kitty or round about without the slightest danger of getting wrecked.

The longer the block from the mat the more reason for playing the bowl from an outside and not an inside position. For short, medium, and very short blocks on the line of the normal draw, or in the eye, always stand up towards the front of the mat, as shown in Fig. 16, and play inside the obstruction.

Sometimes the position of a block is so acute as to make it expedient to narrow down your effort as much as is possible. Look at Fig. 18. The position on the green is that a short bowl, not in the draw, but in the drive, or firm shot, prevents the player from getting contact with the head. He has no 'line,' and that obstruction appears to loom larger and get in his passage.

So he must resort to mat tactics. By placing the left foot ahead of the right, as shown, with both skirting the edge of the mat but just inside it, the player gets a new line to his objective. Standing quite normally, his line is closed, and from a lying down position he could not hit a bowl on the jack wth a rifle, much less with the use of his arm.

By the means explained the player's right arm is away inches to the right of the base, thus giving him a line well past the blocking bowl. It is right to point out here how our systematised education stands to us in such an emergency as with this difficult block. Our grip, our stance and delivery, our power over the bowl with the thumb grip, giving direction, all assist us in making that track past the block, and to

Fig. 16—The bowler is here seen standing up to within 12 in (30.48 cm) of the top left-hand corner of the mat, for the purpose of getting inside a short block, half-way up the green on forehand. By so doing, the player is enabled to gain so much green advantage at the mat end that his bowl can pass within a foot inside of the block and reach the head without being narrow. The player here is not foot-faulting, nor in Figs. 13, 15, 17 and 18.

Fig. 17.—The illustration here represents a player so manipulating the mat on the forehand that he can get past a block half-way up the green, on the outside. The white line indicates where the bowl should be grassed, wide out on the right of the mat.

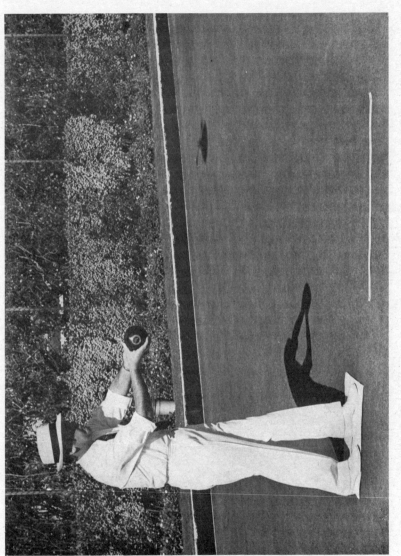

Fig. 18—Here the player is blocked by a bowl right in line with the kitty, making it impossible to get past with a straight drive. In this instance only a fast, straight drive would reach the head; a 'bender' would certainly get wrecked. By playing the feet as shown, on the extreme edge of the mat, a new line is obtained, and the bowl passes up the white line and the block is missed by 6 to 8 inches. A difficult shot, nevertheless.

Fig. 19—The backhand is here blocked by a bowl well up towards the head, and it becomes necessary to get inside of it without being narrow. To accomplish that, the player must stand as shown, well to right-hand side of mat. This gives him 'virgin country', and the bowl passes naturally inside of the block.

take all the bias off in the effort. Note particularly how handicapped are those who only command the bend or firm shot, and invariably crash.

The mat is a base, a protection from heelers, toers, turf strippers, and surface spoilers generally, and, like the D in billiards, and the crease in cricket, all operations must be confined so that one foot remains wholly within the area of its borders, either on it, or immediately above it at the moment of delivery.

Not alone useful and necessary is this illustration (Fig. 18). For drawing on short ends, or getting inside or outside of a bowl in any position, this method is used largely in all my games. It, and similar efforts or poses, is the only time when we dispense with our habitual stance.

In all efforts to defeat blocks it must be understood that great judgment is necessary. I work from the top edge on both sides, in the centre, and from the extreme back, according to the lie of the obstruction. One of the most difficult blocks to defeat is that of a bowl right on the maximum point of the draw; what we have learned to term the 'shoulder.'

Any effort too narrow or too wide is useless unless the obstruction is just missed, and nobody cares to take the risk of getting so close to being stopped. With such a lie it is always best to try getting inside the obstruction, and Fig. 19 will give us the key. 'What we sow, that will we also reap,' comes into the picture again.

Note the position of the feet on this illustration (Fig. 19). The block amounts to one as described, lying right in the normal draw, on the 'shoulder' of the line. By grassing the bowl from that right-hand corner we save at least two feet of green—narrow it down—and the result will assuredly demonstrate itself at the other end and defeat the block quite comfortably.

Many players resort to what they term 'standing up' their bowls, but the claim almost invariably comes from those with narrow ones, who, when invited to 'stand up' something taking 10 ft (3 m) or more, can never be coaxed into trying their skill in doing so. Learn to beat the mat; what you may be able to accomplish at 'standing them up' will only serve to undo one or more of the other necessary parts, and my advice

71

is to 'always do the same thing' in delivery. Attempts to stand them up beget jerking and twisting the wrist.

Stepping out with the left foot (for right-handers) while the bowl is being brought back is faulty as a principle and fatal to balance. Observe the soldier on the march. His right hand and arm go forward at the same instant as his left leg and foot. Thus Nature provides him with that balance essential to walking. Face a mirror and see yourself walking up to it. Apply this, then, to your game of bowls fundamentals, and make all the limb-movements harmonise as one action. Those players who plant the left foot forward and swing back, two separate actions, pinch many of their bowls, and so run narrow on the back hand. Try the action, and note also how much out of plumb your body is with the lines mentioned elsewhere.

PREJUDICE ON BLOCK SHOT IS DEAD

WHEN will single-handed bowlers and skippers cease to give away advantages, and protect their hard-earned shots on a head?

The singles man has only himself to think of, but the skip owes it to his men, who have built up a winning head, to endeavour to keep out the other skip's two bowls.

Not so very many years ago, a short block was unknown, except on the part of only two players. Now, as an old song says, 'Everybody's doing it!' I refer to Australia.

At Melbourne, two teams were playing the semi-final of Country Week fours.

Look at the diagram with this article, representing a full-length jack.

With three ends to go, one led by three points, when the end shown was being played.

Side using plain disc bowls lay six and the skip drew a seventh with his last.

The run to the jack on the backhand was as wide open as goal posts on a football field.

Anything narrow would have been wrecked on short bowls.

The cross disc skip drew the

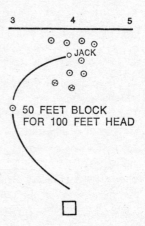

72

actual with his last bowl, so the others were left with seven addled eggs.

After the game I asked the skip: 'Why didn't you put in a block to hold those seven shots?'

He replied: 'I did try to, my intention being to stop about 6 ft or 8 ft (2-3 m) short of head.'

Risking a rebuff from the gentle indictment, I ventured further:

'That kind of block is not only a waste of the bowl, but a guide; rarely are they of any use.'

The short, or half-way-up block, is a winner; the three-quarter or nearer the head, a loser. Why?

Players, and players' temperaments, vary. None care to go too close to a block, either on the inside or outside of it.

The inside attempt would soon cut across, narrow, and the outside, run wide.

I have discovered that a good many top-notch champion players can be trapped with the block.

With these, and numberless others, there is a deep reason. Great players as those men are, the short, effective block grows to an enormous size in their vision. The reason?

It's in their eye, because it is a fixed habit of thought with them. Their subconscious minds cause a Size 5 (5") bowl to become something akin to this.

Partner and self met a noted pair in the ABC finals at Perth. Scenting a case for the block in the skip, I dropped one half-way up.

Running up 25-17, we made that score for that reason.

He crashed into 14 short blocks, because, to use his own words, 'they looked as big as galvanised tanks.'

During that debacle his fixed habit of thought made them that big.

It would be a mistake to assume that there are a great many of these chronic cases, but you won't find them if you don't seek them.

Therefore, it is pleasing to me, as pioneer of the block shot in this country, that at last it has become popular.

All British and other works on the game are fanatically opposed to blocks. Here is one of many warnings they issue:

'In the eyes of the expert, a block is rather laughable.'

But another says (with truth): 'Its effectiveness is due more to a disturbing psychological influence.'

Ironically, it is the expert players who allow such a small object to cause them to shy off near approach to a block. It is we who laugh, when the British player crashes into one of these 'laughable' obstructions.

SHOWMEN THRILL THE GALLERIES

HERE is another angle on the drive, a department that, despite perpetual 'floggings' from its detractors, is as indispensable as the air we breathe.

The showman in any sport always makes appeal. And more so if the showmanship is natural. Anyone with a well-balanced mentality will admit this.

To watch a natural showman at bowls is mentally wholesome, invigorating, stimulating, and only a hypochondriac would fail to appreciate him.

Unbalanced outlooks there will always be, regarding the subject as 'flash,' or 'playing to the gallery.'

The further the drab, morbid, old-time, all-draw and no variety species is left behind, the better for the game's popularity, not to say welfare.

Even the 'gallery' players have their value, but blessed is he who is not conscious of so performing.

CALCULATION, AN ACCESSORY

STANDARD greens at the moment are 110 ft (33.5 m), 120 ft (36.5 m), 125 ft (38 m) but the 120 ft (38 m) predominate. On the 120-ft (38 m) green, 108 ft (33 m) is the maximum playing length. The medium is 87 ft (26.5 m) and the minimum 66 ft (20 m).

From the front of the mat (or six-feet mark) to the jack on the 108 ft (33 m) length, if the bowl ran straight up a line, it would take 81 revolutions, using a $5\frac{1}{8}$ bowl.

Allowing for an eight-feet draw, it would make approximately 84 revolutions. From the front of the mat to the 87-ft (26.5 m) mark, in a straight line, the same bowl would make 65 revolutions, while it would make (approx.) $67\frac{1}{2}$ in the draw.

From the front of the mat to the jack on the 66 ft (20 m)

mark, $49\frac{1}{2}$ turns of the bowl would take place, in straight line, and $51\frac{1}{2}$ in the draw.

These figures might appear to be of no value, but to the player who studies figures in relation to length, and works to calculation, they loom large.

The same figures and reasoning apply to the lesser lengths, of course. So that, although one bowl runs four feet-odd (about a metre) further than the other, both are the same distance from the white. An excellent margin to work on when playing to figures.

If you are playing to the full length (108 ft or 33 m), and get per medium of elevation (weight of the bowl theory) 83 revolutions out of your bowl, that bowl would be on the white.

If you only get 81 you obtain a good result. In each case your bowl would be a good length one. One thing is certain, the man who plays to calculation—what he does at the mat end—has advantage over the average exponent.

RHYTHM IN DELIVERY

CONTROL of the bowl is dependent on the actions of the body. Any man not 'too far gone,' who desires to get on the right track, should make a point of watching a good match, where the players are above the ordinary.

Even there he will find a multiplicity of styles and methods, mostly the product of the individual; but a study enables him to get down to something concrete himself.

In nearly all of the many I have handled, and who have had previous experience, I have had to 'bring them upstanding' in one particular direction.

The bad habit of stepping out with the left foot first, while the bowl is being brought back from the poise, or stance, is paramount among 95 per cent of those playing the game, and is very difficult to cure with chronics.

As mentioned elsewhere, we should take our cue from the soldier on the march, and apply it to our game.

Notice how, as the right arm moves forward, the left foot steps in uniformity at the same time. And so the action of the left foot should be delayed until the bowl is brought back to extreme, and then the right arm and left leg go forward simultaneously.

Thus the actions or movements demand the following preliminaries:—Playing on either hand: Heels together, toes apart, one foot facing kitty.

Spine bent comfortably, but not strained, and both hands holding the bowl. That constitutes the poise.

After concentrating on the green required, and judging the strength needed, the player goes off, as it were.

Here the vital point presents itself: It is at this particular moment that he mostly sticks out that left foot prematurely.

The correct and balanced method is to delay left leg movement until the bowl is on the forward swing. Then rhythm in delivery comes into its own with the forward swing.

All limbs and the spine act in unison, the left hand falling naturally on the left knee, bent to receive it. The whole process spells balance.

The watchword of this treatise is simplicity. Don't try to make the bowl do things, but deliver it on an even keel and give it a chance to do its work. Leave 'standing them up' to the straight-bowl brigade. Either the bowl or you must rule—let it be you. When it runs past the head, yards strong, or stops yards short, the bowl definitely rules. Only when you can control its actions can you be definitely on top. Crossing the legs to beat a block is a science not well understood. Don't criticise it as flash: go out after it.

LINE OF LEAST RESISTANCE

IF you claim to be anything in the nature of a skilful bowler, the following study will be found worth your while:

A layer of odds challenges you to put your skill up against his money. You accept. The first problem set is a jack nine inches from a bowl, 87 ft (26.5 m) up the green.

'What odds that I cannot beat that shot bowl on the draw?' you ask. 'Five to one,' replies the layer.

'What odds that I cannot remove bowl or kitty?' is the next proposition. 'You have to play odds on.' Note the vast difference between the prices he offers. Why?

Simply because one shot is ever so much easier to accomplish than the other. His 5 to 1 on a running green (13-15 sec) would be termed cramped by expert layers.

What lesson, then, do we learn from these interrogatories? A good one, to be sure.

When a head is big, and the proposition five to one against drawing the shot, why select the latter, when an even money, or odds-on, is there for your choice?

If we take the layer's view of the possibilities, or probabilities, which is the sound view, then we should not hesitate to take the line of least resistance and deal with the head without delay—despite what non-drive experts have to offer against that procedure.

CONCENTRATION INDISPENSABLE

CONCENTRATION is a term we apply to the study of a position, shot, stroke or problem in sport, and in bowls it is particularly applicable. We could no more play billiards well if we dispensed with concentration and indulged in conversation than we could add up columns of figures correctly while talking to somebody. And it is quite certain that nobody can play bowls of a competitive kind with a desire to win without having his mind on the job in front of him.

We can dispense with the term as it applies to other sport, and content ourselves with a study of how it affects our game for good or ill. In rink play, whether social or otherwise, there are always some in the party of eight who must talk. A player's hearing is never so keen as when it comes to his turn to concentrate upon a shot—he hears every whisper.

In singles play, likewise, we often strike the loquacious opponent who means well by his chatter, but who knows no better; and whether it be a championship game or just a roll-up, he would always run second. To him the term concentration means that the other fellow is one of those who take the game too seriously.

What is concentration, after all—say, in bowls? I can best explain it as it presents itself to me. During the course of a game it is considered bad form, or taste, to carry on in silence entirely, and it is seldom done; but there are times when it must be put up with, and we will assume that this is one of them.

Forget the surroundings, whether they be congenial, hostile, or strictly neutral, and allow the mind to dwell upon the business of the game. When the opponent or opponents take the mat, or ask questions, or receive directions, we have to be in it, noting any tendency to avoid a particular hand, or shun an order from a skip. We must concentrate on these weaknesses, and store them away in our mental warehouse.

We also have to memorise greatly, remembering the strength or weakness of our previous shot, how the hand played, and if the green was running true to that particular length. It is often necessary to vary one's stance to get a different course out of your bowl, if the surface is tricky, and runs across or keeps out—and all these things call for close concentration.

I have the reputation for extreme silence when playing, except when directing or asking questions of the marker in singles. To the initiated the reason is apparent, for it should be known that one cannot allow the mind to attempt excursions in different directions at the same time. The brain of a good player at bowls is always working during a hard game, especially he who plays to figures.

Let us get down to actual procedure in concentration. Outside of a close study of all things affecting or related to the game, we have to keep our memory green concerning correct methods. We take up our bowl, and remind ourselves that we must grip it correctly; we know that if we want to get it away sweetly we must do that, and also stand correctly.

We have to think quickly, and act quickly, as over-concentration is trying to the nerves, looks ugly, and is altogether not desirable. So that within a few seconds we must do all those things we have been taught, dispensing with none and dovetailing one into the other.

Our amount of green must be right, our strength good, and our step in keeping with the run of the surface. All these things spell concentration, and demonstrate its value and necessity. Ever-changing lengths, change of wind, slowing down of green owing to shadows, or lateness of the hour; change for the better with a drying surface in late morning play, so is it any wonder that we have to concentrate deeply?

To relax in this connection is often fatal, and how many games are lost and how many sides or players lose touch through relaxing their minds and indulging in conversation? In social bowls we can usually tell who are present, and give them some attention on the banks; but, personally, I must confess, when playing singles, that admirers or non-admirers may be seated at either end without my being conscious of the fact.

While murmurings on the bank may be audible, acquire the 'not interested' habit. In short, keep the mind on the game; keep the brain working towards the end to which you have set yourself the task of attaining; and ever concentrate.

Players undoubtedly lose many points by a too-hurried procedure between poise and judgment of length. Every bowl has its value, and the truth of what I propound here can be found when the player is up against it and is compelled to take extra precautions.

I have written 'Think quickly and act quickly,' but that does not mean sacrificing the value of any bowl and getting rid of it without the satisfaction of knowing or feeling that you are getting full value for your effort. Take your time. You pay if you lose. Visit the head if in doubt.

NON-CONFIDENCE AN ACQUIRED COMPLEX

INABILITY to stand up to the strain of things, from various angles, is nothing against a man. It is just something that is very difficult to define, for, whereas many of our best players unflinchingly, and with amazing courage, faced death a score of times in the wars, a large percentage of them would fail with the strain of a big game at bowls, billiards, golf and other sport. Every man is a problem unto himself, and must depend upon himself to eradicate any tendency towards funk, or what we more often refer to as 'displaying the yellow streak.'

Let it first be understood that no man is entirely free from this trait in his make-up. I can recall the times in my earlier career when that creepy feeling about the region of the abdomen, the short breath during the first few ends, and the consequent loss—at least temporarily—of control had a marked effect upon my game.

I soon learned that, if not eradicated, all the knowledge, all the practice, and all the ordinary roll-up efficiency would be discounted by that something that asserted itself immediately the real strain was on. It gave me much thought, and no small amount of concern after a defeat, to know that I could have done much better had it not been for a tendency to 'towel it' at times.

But, just as I beat it, so can the average player, although there will remain those who will never do so, because they accept the inferiority complex as something that is beyond their control, and make matters worse by resigning themselves to their fate. I know many fine, first-class club players who would be insulted if told what one could tell them, and who would indignantly exclaim: 'What! me? Not on your life!'

Much better for a man to sit down and ask himself: 'I wonder if I am?' Indeed, he should accept it that he is a bit inclined that way, and to then put the acid test on himself by finding out how he feels in that connection the next time he is in a big match—singles, particularly—and when opposed to a high-class opponent.

It is a generally accepted fact that a much too large percentage of bowlers 'turn it in' as soon as they see the draw for a singles championship and enter upon the first round—particularly if meeting a good man in the initial stage. The greatest problem State selectors have to solve before definitely taking in a new man is whether he will stand the strain.

Experience has taught that known good players fail, not because of the want of experience, but because, to put it mildly, they are 'yellow,' and can't help themselves; yet this might apply only in the sporting sense. The same men would be strong in other directions, where the man who is never affected in sport would be weak.

Many an early break is obtained on an opponent from the fact that he had not 'settled down' early. That settling down means a nervous approach and want of confidence; that chin-in-the-air, the-bigger-they-are-the-heavier-they-fall demeanour is missing, and all the time the other fellow either knows it or assumes it. When two such meet, it is a first-class tragedy and the survival of the fittest.

It is very necessary that a player carry a big heart into the game, and I would advise beginners, and those early in the sport, to approach matches, and events other than social games, in the same calm spirit, as a practice roll-up by themselves.

That nervousness that we call 'the streak' can almost wholly be got rid of, as, after all, strong will-power is all that is necessary.

To admit of an inferiority complex—especially to the world —makes the problem more difficult. Beginners, particularly, must acquire determination early, and never look upon any proposition as beyond them. We hear and know of many in all sport who have a name for being 'chicken-hearted,' etc— just another term for our subject. Once rid of that want of confidence in one's self, and the cancer is beaten, if not really killed.

It's a great thing to know one's man. If you know your man you can do things that otherwise you would not care to risk. Every bowler has his peculiarities, and most have their weaknesses, and to become a winner these must be exploited.

Most players are aware of these things in their fellow clubmen, but only those who have played for years in the big events know anything about the outsiders.

That is the outstanding reason why the younger generation should go out after as much experience as possible. Like many people, I do not condemn a colt of only a few months' tuition (provided he was properly taught) for entering for big events.

Every bowler is more or less pregnable; he can be beaten, and in beating him, of course, I do not include 'pointing' on him.

Look for his bad hand and block his good. Make him play to the back often if you have a drive and he hasn't. Thus he gives you a big handicap by having to waste many bowls that he might otherwise use against you in the draw.

Some men can't stand 'one in the eye,' when you have placed a good block. Others can't play short ends, particularly on fast greens (16-18 sec). Many can't play the long ones too well, while others get worried if you take the mat up to the centre of the green.

In short, get to know your man inside the club and out of it. To be successful you must possess a policy, even though it might be the same as your opponent's. Many players win hard games with their heads. Block an opponent's preference hand. It keeps the points down.

SOME TRIBUTARIES

WHEN a course of instruction has been absorbed, it would be a mistake to suppose that there is nothing else to be learned. What has to be learned in addition, however, can only come with experience: the finishing touches to a bowler's education when he is at last able to say that he can expect to get results, and more than hold his own with the best. It doesn't matter much what order we take the many little points I propose to dwell upon, for they have little relation to system or the combination.

Very few greens are perfectly level and draw equally on both hands, unfortunately, and in most cases a wily player will use his head, and, without being in a position where he has no choice, take the hand that is playing, or working, reliably. Very often it pays well to leave a hand almost entirely alone, especially when directing the three men in a fours game. How often do we see bad results when players are forced on to a faulty hand, particularly when that bad hand is not the pet one for that particular player, or players—for, in spite of themselves, every bowler has a preference, be it ever so slight.

After the final of a classic someone remarked to me: 'I noticed throughout the game that you never followed the course of your opponent's bowl up the green, except on rare occasions; do you think that course advisable?' I certainly do. In a long game of 31 up, which usually runs into three hours, there is a big strain on the eyes, as well as the nerves, and the latter are very closely related to the former.

What my friend actually noticed was this: I invariably follow the course of my own bowl, right up to the point where it comes to rest, but not so my opponent's—except when I want to block him with my next. Then I fix on a spot his bowls have traversed, and make that my kitty, provided, of course, he has not beaten me to the shot. Following the course of the opponent's bowl brings unnecessary eyestrain, prevents the nerves from having a temporary respite, and keeps the individual at a tension much higher than is good for him. By long practice I have come to know—guess if you like—just when the other fellow's bowl is within 10 or 12 ft (3-4 m) of the head. If it is very open I don't even bother to look at all.

82

That temporary rest is very calm-producing to the temperament, and one lasts better.

One can best demonstrate an object lesson on the evils of chopping and changing about—playing different hands with successive bowls—by a description of a semi-final game witnessed in Sydney in the State Championship. One man had come from behind brilliantly for no other reason than that he kept to the same hand going one way, and again kept to one hand when playing the other. He was a shot in the lead, 28-27, at what proved to be the last end.

Dropping 12 feet short with his first, his opponent got one close, and then the fatal mistake occurred. I remarked, 'Foolish man!' at the time, when I saw him twist to the hand he had avoided with such good judgment to gain his points. His bowl did not come in, and was wide. The other man drew another. Then he switched back to the original hand, and placed one nine inches just beyond kitty. His opponent drew close, and, thinking discretion the better part, he placed a bowl at the back. Now here was where his chopping about became his undoing. With the last bowl the 27 man—it was 31 up—played up and pushed him out for four and game.

My advice is to keep pegging away on the hand that is working, and which the player knows will be reliable in running. If you are a skip, don't chop your men about, as often the previous bowl is a yard or so short, or strong, and, knowing the hand, the player will take the bit off, or add to it, and give you a better result.

To those who have not been long in the game it becomes difficult to size up an opponent until you have had at least one game against him, but one game should be sufficient to discover his strong as well as his weak points. A very large percentage of bowlers have a weakness for either long or short ends, and some make themselves particularly transparent by their persistency in throwing their pet length. Again, a personal experience will enable me to demonstrate:

In one of the big classic quarter finals in Sydney, I noticed the players in the next rink, and, taking into account the possibility of having to meet the winner, took a mental note of their tactics. Subsequently I was in the position to know that my opponent had particularly avoided the 'baby' ends, and at about the sixth, after he had got well into the long-step swing that had enabled him to win previously, I gave him a 66'r. and added two fours and a three before he could get back to the shorts. I merely quote that as showing the wisdom of studying your man.

Some players work on the knowledge that they can put an opponent off his length, or prevent him from exploiting one, by engaging him in conversation, or taking him in for refreshment as often as he will go. On these five points I don't propose to dwell. Placing the front of the mat in the rough is another example of 'generalship' I need not take up space with, except to remark that the freemasonry among bowlers becomes a lost art at such times, even with reputedly good sportsmen. The man who makes a point of displaying indignation if his sportsmanship is adversely referred to, is usually found wanting when the acid test comes.

Most humans are gamblers, in spite of themselves or their outlook. The average Australian is no exception. For all time a controversy has raged on the drawbacks as well as the value of the drive shot in bowls. As one who has exploited the shot, I am competent to write about its values and drawbacks, and yet another personal experience will help us to conclusions.

Playing a capable opponent in the Victorian Singles final at Brighton, he began very accurately, and compelled me to resort to the heavy shots. Prior to the game, a well-known player, who was taking a fatherly interest in me, came up and remarked: 'You have done splendidly, but I think you drive too much!'

I was a baby in experience, but my reply was: 'Whatever my policy has been, it has got me in the final, and I don't think it would be wise to change it at this stage.' What he said further need not be mentioned, but the Press notes appearing the following day read: 'The winner displayed very sound judgment in using the drive shot when to draw to inches on the keen surface was much the longer odds.'

So now get back to our lesson: Know when to drive and when to leave it alone. I say very emphatically that in the long run the draw, draw, draw, pays much bigger dividends. It is entirely a matter of the player's judgment, and no two players are alike either in their views or their ability to sum up a position. Drawing and sticking to the hands that play are keys to the games. When to drive fast and when to firm is just a similar proposition, and depends upon the ability and view of the man behind the bowl.

It is a commonly accepted fact that most bowlers cannot draw accurately after a drive or a series of drives. What is the reason? I have often pointed out that after the shadows of 50 have thrown themselves over a man, his heart accelerates to a greater degree than in former years, and the older he gets the more pronounced becomes this condition. He is called upon to 'save,' or decides to do so, after a hefty effort, and, with the excitement consequent upon missing, and the fact that 'a bundle' is lying against him, the old ticker has increased its beats by many.

That condition affects his whole body, his nervous system, and his muscles particularly. He picks up his second bowl while in this state, and the result is that he is strong—the natural outcome. Now there is a remedy, and a sure and safe one. Before even picking up that succeeding bowl—it might be at any part of a game in singles—relax the muscles by dropping the arms to the side and allow them to settle. At the same time, drop the mentality by not worrying about what you didn't do, and take a casual look round at Nature—at the flower-beds, or up at the clouds—and you will walk on to the mat normal, and mostly succeed.

VIEWING THE HEAD

SOME real 'bank-seat echoes' float over occasionally, and it makes quite good reading to get these reflections from the garden seats. If those who sit around at big matches don't see most of the game, they at least hear most of the gossip, and, if only to correct misconceptions, a recital of some of the happenings that are every-day affairs will not be out of place.

I have occasionally sprinted or hiked to the head in order to view the lie, and these excursions have been adversely commented upon, and wrong conclusions come to regarding their reason.

In the first place, though blessed with good sight, it is sometimes not as clear as it might be, and, more or less, we all suffer in this respect. I often have no confidence in playing blind, and prefer to see the position and the possibilities.

How often does the average player, when arriving at the other end, find it quite different from up there, and, as the rules gives reasonable latitude for looking, why the man on the bank, whose education is not always complete, should comment, or object, or call it 'flash,' is not clear. On top of that, one often misses good 'plants' by failure to know the precise position.

A 'plant' at bowls is often an easy way out of a difficulty, and missed by 95 per cent. At times it is a gift from Heaven, and, when turned to good account, mostly regarded as a fluke by the onlookers. He would be a poor sort of a sport who would keep going to the jack end for the purpose of putting his opponent off, or any such rubbish. Only a small-minded man would make such an accusation, besides being deficient in bowls intelligence.

Another echo is one concerning measuring for shot. It is often asked: 'What's the umpire for? Why doesn't he do the measuring?' Onlooker players who are not conversant with rules and procedure should refrain from making such interrogations.

The supposed umpire is the scorer or marker. He has nothing whatever to do with the game, except to act as a convenience to answer questions about the lie and to straighten the kitty.

Where he is umpire he still has no power until the players fail to agree, and is then brought into the picture by them to decide. That is as it should be. The game belongs to the players. The procedure in measuring is for one to do it, and then, if satisfied that it is against him, say 'one down,' or hand the measure to his opponent for his decision. If differing, the umpire is then called in.

PERSONALITY SKIPS

PERSONALITY skips are the gate-crashers of the sport. They are the dunces in the ranks of beau monde artists, and specialise in that section. All the same, they are indispensable units of all social bowls battalions and the glow-worm in the dark night of business and professional fretfulness.

But that is where their usefulness ends. Unfortunately for the game, they are often found where the glamour atmosphere gives place to stern realism. Many are given jobs in the hard competitive arena by short-sighted selectors, on the assumption that they can get more out of their men than others of superior knowledge and playing ability.

The combination of personal quality and playing ability in a skip is a rare winning double, the second leg usually being of the cork variety. Just as you would not seek hardening of the arteries in an artificial limb, neither should you expect the personal skip, minus those indispensable essentials, to succeed where his so-called rivals fail.

Viewed broadly, the efficient and knowledgeable skip who fails to extract the various shots from particular players, would say that the shots are not there to extract. Alibis are instruments used by the inefficient, and they are many and varied.

It is largely psychological and the presence of an inferiority complex, that few, if any, care to admit. Don't advertise weaknesses by declaring that you can't do your best for this or that man—remedy the defects.

SOMETHING LACKING

Do you ever feel that there is something lacking in your game? That you are not getting the results you should? Are you disappointed in yourself and feel that you are capable of better things, and yet don't get anywhere in the game?

Many thousands of bowlers are asking themselves these questions daily. It is a fact that a much too large percentage lack that finish which makes for success.

Follow the trend of the big championships, and note how many men you know as good players fall out when the acid is put upon their skill. Frequently one of these looks a sure thing to go further, and then fades out of the event with a very small score.

Just as a wise man allows himself to be periodically looked over by a medical man, so he should look himself over and try to discover where lies that weakness that keeps him out of the last eights, or fours, not to mention finals.

We have far too many near champions, just near enough to be uncertain how they will perform next.

Every player must work out his own salvation. There is no cure done up in small packets and sold at cut prices. Every man should draw up his own chart, mark off the weak spots in red ink, and discontinue to imagine that the last effort was not his true form.

Something lacking! What a wealth of meaning in those two words! And nobody can decipher them better than the man himself, if he only would.

Personal experiences are the best examples I can hand to the readers of this book.

My first success in the game was the Victorian State Championship. When leaving the clubhouse at 8.30 on the morning of the first day, the secretary said: 'We are holding a Welch Main at 2 o'clock, will I put you in?'

I stammered embarrassingly: 'But I'm playing in the State Singles!' The secretary laughed, and those around laughed louder and added to my embarrassment; but when I failed to return, and was still playing at 6.30 to win the day there, the thought uppermost in my mind was: 'Where would a man be if it were not for confidence in himself?' So that, whatever circumstance you may find yourself having to face, do so with the confidence that you will succeed.

Applause is sweet music to the player who earns it. It is cheap, inspiring, and begets comradeship. Be discreet in your approbation, however. If you applaud any old shot merely to encourage, your team never knows the genuine article from the brumby.

Too much emphasis cannot be placed upon the warning to clubs not to elect personality, non-player, or good knowledge of the game men as coaches, unless, by achievement in the field—and abundance of it at that—they command the right to be considered eligible to teach others!

Remarkable as it may seem, the hand that is playing early in the day (or hands) often becomes the hand that is not playing later in the day. This was forcibly brought home to me in a hard game of 31, beginning at 3 o'clock. The game, which lasted $3\frac{1}{2}$ hours, became different on both hands, about 5 o'clock. The cause of this was (and will always be) that the grass followed the sun as it moved further west, and whereas what was the straighter hand became the greater drawing side, and vice versa.

KNOWING YOUR MAN

ONLY those skips who have been through the searching school of experience are competent to write in the strain contained in this article.

It is these men, who have had every conceivable class of player to study, and who have been able to take mental note of the vagaries of temperament. These are the recorders, or historians, who are able to place bowlers for what they have been worth.

Experience has taught them that few, if any, club men can be correctly judged by what is seen of them on the local green. There it is difficult to fault them, and often, in such games as pennant, they apparently stand up to it quite satisfactorily.

But it has been proved, time and again, that seventy-five per cent put into interstate ranks or classic events fail to produce anything like the form they have shown in games that call for less of the acid test.

State selectors, and even club match committees, have been compelled to drop some of their best men after one trial. The ability is there, but standing up to the glare of the footlights is another thing.

The trouble is that they must be given that first trial before they are found out, and further trouble of another kind sets in after the discovery. The most astonished of all are these very players who have to be disrated.

All this is accentuated when they are returned to their previous positions in the pennants or local matches, for invariably the known ability re-presents itself, to complicate matters and give them fresh alibis.

How, then, does the skip, who has been through the mill, stand in relation to these subjects whom he would not take out into big events again? He blames them, they have to find an answer, and point to him as the fly in the ointment.

We have to accept the conclusions of these men of experience much as it may appear distasteful. The cold fact is that, firstly, a very large percentage do not stand up to the strain of big events.

Secondly, knowing that their reputations are at stake, the first human impulse is to look round for a way out. In this process, they unkindly shoulder on to the skip some peculiarity as the reason for the lapse or non-production of their known good game. This produces a doubt in the minds of their friends, and the badly-informed fall for it.

It can be laid down as standard, that players who avow they can't play for this or that man are victims of that 'something' the author prefers to leave to others to define. Match players are born, not made, some of the best in the land failing when the occasion is outstanding. The moral to all this is to know the men you would take out when selecting a side.

Many bowlers are conscious of the fact that they favour a particular hand. Many are not. Some know it and won't admit such to be the case. Pig-headedness in these things retards progress, and don't throw any smokescreens. Get out on the green and take practice exclusively on the weak hand.

Attempts to beat short-blocks, when they are palpably dead in the 'running way,' is a losing game. Most players make the attempt rather than admit defeat. Say to yourself: 'You win!' and take the other hand. Often, playing 'on the timber,' brings good results.

When the forward swing of the right (or left) arm begins, five distinct parts of the anatomy come into action—or should —simultaneously. They are: The swinging arm, the left (or right) leg, the other leg, the spine, and the drop of the left (or right) hand on to the knee. All this must be one action.

Don't be a law unto yourself at bowls. Model your game on the correct movements as set out in the textbook, and results, other things being equal, must come.

Little things are more than helpful. Before beginning a singles match, take your bearings (points of aim, approximately, note the windage, etc) and mark with chalk the six feet distance at both ends. Then 'land-buyer' scorers with long legs won't be able to step seven to eight feet before laying the kitty at their toes.

INCONSISTENCY IN LENGTH

ONE of the difficulties of the beginner is to become efficient in length, especially on keen surfaces (15-17 sec). The keener the running the more difficult he finds it to play two bowls alike.

It is not generally understood that the state of the green for the time being is a factor governing good or bad length.

The faster the green the shorter the step for the various lengths, and the slower the surface the longer the step when the kitty is thrown nearer the ditch.

You will often notice, when somebody is apparently floundering on a fast-running surface, that he fails with the varying lengths because he always takes the same stride. Watch him put a bowl 6 ft (2 m) short, in attempting to get up with the next, run 6-8 ft (2-3 m) too strong. The step you take should synchronise with the swing you use.

Note the effect of short step, keen green play when the player is a recognised expert at the game. He has control all the time, and if he drops one short or overruns the head he immediately corrects it.

Adopt one step, or stride, for a particular length. If you know anything about the elevation theory, you will begin a four-bowl game by elevating to a certain judged level. If the first effort is a reasonably good one, you will drop or raise that extra bit, so that the next is a better one.

But you must do the same thing with all your bowls—the same length of step, the same easy, non-jerk swing, and the same elevation when you strike it. Thus you become mechanical and machine-like. It is the man who does four different things with four different bowls who can't control his length.

If you take a chute out on to the green and place the first bowl on an even keel, it will run to a given spot. Place a second one in the same way, and it will finish within an inch of the first.

But cant the next one slightly and give it an inch less elevation, and you will be astonished how short it will finish. Now take a fourth and place it a little differently from the others, with the correct elevation, and see where it will run also.

Therefore, if a machine will show bad results in relation to length and draw, what must you expect from the human arm, which is not mechanically constructed, and is affected by temperament and other things impossible in the machine? The latter has no balance to consider, and no short or long step. Therefore, it is your job to imitate the machine, and like it, do the same thing each time with your bowl—only varying in the matter of elevation until the correct length is struck.

SHORT BOWLS SYMBOLS OF DEFEAT

THEY shut the entrances to the head.

Instead of being positional assets they become encumbrances to the side or individual.

Such bowls, if very short, seldom get knocked up and prevent the skip driving into the position.

One at the back is worth 10 in the way, as not a kitty in 100 comes matwards when struck.

When a player so handicaps his side he actually makes a fifth man in a four for the opposition.

They are a distinct menace and handicap to a versatile skipper.

The game embraces 'ports,' 'entrances,' and 'channels,' that have to be navigated by the last bowl of an end.

Such bowls, if consistently not up, point to the senders as nervous subjects, afraid of over-running. Much better to over-run.

Not being touchers, they become monuments of impotence when the jack is forced into the ditch.

There are many other negative aspects to the shorts.

Many players are noted obstructionists, and in due course are regarded by skips and selectors as chronic, and are dropped.

How many bowls, seemingly useless as too strong, come into the count picture in a game of 25 ends?

On the other hand, the short and shiftless remain for what they are—neither useful nor ornamental.

Never handicap a forceful third or skip by dropping in the way. This advice is given to both leaders and second men.

FAST SURFACES SHOW UP WEAKNESSES

LENGTH control. Fiery or racing greens (19-21 sec) make most players look foolish. Bowling loses its art, skill and charm on slow (9-10 sec) or narrow-running greens.

Those who don't vary their step for the different lengths cannot be consistent, and are only occasional winners of games.

Short and minimum lengths on a fast surface demand finger and wrist action, plus a short step from the mat.

92

A medium, short three-quarter, and three-quarter, call for finger—wrist—half-arm action, with slightly longer step.

A full length only brings the hand-to-shoulder, known as 'the pendulum' swing into the picture. Suicidal for 'baby' lengths.

Players who bowl by always taking the same length step, as many do, lose control and length, and are usually caught on the short ends.

If a bowler cannot manage short or medium lengths, the faults are to be found in the above lesson. Without touch and balance he must fail when opposed to those who command these essentials.

HOW WEIGHT SPELLS CONTROL

SUPPOSING that my elevation with first bowl lands me, say, 6 ft (2 m) short or 6 ft (2 m) strong. 'What then?' you will ask.

By raising, or lowering, to be sure! The first bowl for any length is the range-finder, and if you strike it correctly (approximately), you can then say to yourself: 'I have standardised that, and must try to do the same thing with my next three.'

This art of doing the same thing, of course, is the key to the theory of elevation, and playing bowls to figures, as I have advocated over the years.

Further to the science that the weight does it: If you drop the bowl back from your elevation point the same distance behind as it was in front of you, and it is, say, a three pounds drop, it must be an unbroken three pounds throughout. No use a three pounds backward swing if you add to it in the forward swing.

LITTLE THINGS COUNT

UNIFORM conditions are first cousins to standardisation. In nearly every kind of sport similar conditions govern. Unfortunately, in bowls you get something different almost everywhere you go. It should not be so.

Detail and details are important factors in most things. Having regard to detail in your game assists you materially against an opponent who does not bother about trifles. Life is made up of little things.

Just let me illustrate the gulf between the two. Ditches at end of greens should be provided with layers of sand, so that when a bowl drives the jack into them it would stay put at the precise spot where driven to. Now to the average player these little things mostly go unnoticed, but they are highly important to a side made up of all those who have an interest in the result.

With that preliminary explanation, we can come to the point. Sometimes the ditches are barren and act as though they were box-drains, and as soon as a kitty enters it runs along out of bounds. This condition is not only contrary to the laws of the game, which provide for a layer of loose sand or other suitable material, but it also nullifies the skill of the game, and is distinctly disconcerting and unfair to the man or side bringing off the shot. Also we sometimes find that the face of the bank is so springy that the jack, or even a bowl, will rebound on to the green, thus producing an equally disconcerting and unfair result.

How often do we see a good effort, with a possible three, four, five points to be picked up by a brilliant drive or some other means employed to get the kitty into a certain position in the ditch, rendered useless. Getting it there is often part of the strategy of the game.

MORE ABOUT ELEVATION

PRIOR to perusal of this, look at Fig. 12. Explanations of illustrations a, b and c speak for themselves.

Assuming that we are playing to say, 108 ft (33 m) length, it follows that so many revolutions of the bowl are needed to get alongside the jack.

Let us accept that 86 revolutions are required. Here we need judgment, according to the state of the surface, as to how high or how low the bowl should be held from the ground.

Perfectly upright stance is, of course, ruled out.

It should be ever ruled out from, and has no connection with, the theories or lessons propounded in this book.

All players should 'get over their work,' as most players do in other lines of sport, such as billiards, golf, cricket, croquet, etc.

On the principle that a three pounds weight swing would

get us on the kitty, it must be three pounds all the time. If it is more or less it must be absolutely regular.

Why? Because, if we start with three pounds, say, and jerk to six at the finish, it becomes irregular, the elevation theory disappears from the picture, and bad results follow.

Jerking has no relation to good, consistent bowling. The point to focus upon is that the weight does it. Therefore, standardise regulation of weight in delivery.

If a full length demands a higher elevation of the bowl—as it does—then the weight of swing increases accordingly. Make yourself a human chute, and cause weight to control length, as the testing chute does to a fraction.

The game has been played for centuries all over the world, but no claim for a royal road to the kitty has ever been established. It was doubtful if one could be found. But after intensive study of the elevation possibilities and then putting them into operation, I have proved by results achieved that there is a sure and royal route. For me it has been a trump card.

That a player can be taught to become heartbreakingly mechanical is no longer theory, but cold fact. But there is a provision that must not be lost sight of. He must follow out to the letter the fundamentals and movements set out and covering at least five of the eight points that comprise the combination I teach.

LENGTH IN RELATION TO DELIVERY

IF a player knows that he must get 83 revolutions out of his bowl, to cover a full-length jack throw, he also knows—or should—that the correct non-dump delivery of the bowl, only, will get it there.

Making that correct delivery embraces several considerations. The take-off in front of the mat must be smooth and conducive to imparting that life or spin into the bowl essential to covering the number of revloutions required.

The thudder or dumper, who does not get down sufficiently is the bad or inconsistent length player. And here is a hint to leaders: Carefully select a part of the green to lay the mat, so that those following you have a clean take-off at any point in front of it.

Many matches are lost through a vital or last bowl, losing revolutions that it would not otherwise have lost had it not struck the rough or broken surface. Even a woolly patch of grass will take from four to six revolutions off a bowl.

This spells 'short stuff,' and often a skip is reminded: 'Be up when the shot is against you,' when, as a matter of truth, the fault lies with the mat-layer.

Here again is the lesson of the movement. One cannot expect to control the number of revolutions required to govern a certain length if his delivery is not smooth, rhythmical and regular.

To be smooth, rhythmical, and regular, one must be balanced, and deliver his bowl as Nature teaches him to walk, viz, with the left foot or leg moving at the precise moment and with the right arm. We are writing of right-handers, of course, but the principle is the same with left.

Work to figures in your game. If, on any length, you drop three feet short of the jack (a good bowl mostly), you only lose about two revolutions, and you have four up your sleeve to place another bowl a yard beyond, and still be in the picture.

And here, on the highly important question of length in relation to delivery, I would stress this point: On fast-running (15-17 sec) surfaces dispense with the full-swing delivery for all lengths up to three-quarter, and especially the very shorts.

Hold the bowl at a low elevation (about 18 in or 45 cm in front of your knees), and don't bring it further back than the side of the leg. Use a fingers and thumb, wrist, half-arm action, or sort of scoop, and you thus control the bowl rather than have it controlling you.

BENDING OVER YOUR WORK

PERFECT stance means perfect balance, and there can be no balance with one foot placed ahead of the other and an erect posture. It would quickly become void by the necessary motions following.

You must follow the military dictum, and place your heels together. Then bend your spine naturally, so that your height is lowered about a foot, to get 'over your work'—an important factor. When you step forward, balance is maintained.

The man who bends over his work immediately brings the muscles of his calves to the ready, likewise those of his thighs. In fact, every muscle in his body is on the alert.

If you stand erect without your arms naturally outstretched, with one foot ahead of the other, this being claimed as perfect stance, the spine has to be bent as a first operation, and the arms have to go through one extra motion. Thus there are two more motions required in this stance than in that which I teach.

Also, the muscles of the whole back would be flabby when a player stands erect, but, if bent as I describe, they would be extended and firm. From a health-giving point of view, double the benefit accrues from the positions I propound.

There is only one right way in regard to stance, grip, delivery, etc, but twenty wrong ways, and I am not prepared to concede anything in this connection. A man with most things wrong might occasionally beat the 'all right' man, but the average is heavily on the side of the latter.

CENTRE OF GRAVITY IN BOWLING

CENTRE of gravity: what does it signify? Try to visualise how many things it applies to. You can't walk without it; you can't sit in a tram without it, and there are a hundred other things that make it indispensable. Look at the tight-rope walker, the jockey, the tennis player, the cricketer, and the golfer. Its relation to balance brings it into close relation to bowls, as I will endeavour to demonstrate.

Turn to the illustration, with the article on Grip, Figs. 3, 4 and 5.

If anything is needed to convince sceptics and die-hards that all grips or holds other than the thumb on the running surface are wrong, then this lesson should convince them. It is cold logic to assume that when you are about to turn or spin a round or semi-round object in sending it up a green or pitch, you must closely consider balance.

In bowls, centre of gravity is balance. Many bowlers are impossible, because they miss centre of gravity in their stand, or if they get it at all, it is momentarily, to be lost completely as soon as they make the first movement. It must be maintained throughout.

Look at the photographs (Figs. 3, 4, 5 and 6): One depicts a player balancing the bowl naturally on the ball of the thumb, showing perfect centre of gravity. When he drops the long finger on to the surface and turns the bowl over to play it, he naturally maintains centre.

If the player who goes to the side, or between the disc and the rings, attempts what is shown in the picture, the bowl drops automatically to the ground, because its gravity is not centre. Therefore, he cannot claim to be holding the bowl with due balance.

Now look at the other picture (Fig. 3). It is the same thing from a side view, and does not call for further comment, except that if you draw a straight line from the tip of the thumb to a point right through the disc that is showing it demonstrates how cleanly and completely the bowl is halved, showing control added to its other virtues.

I once had a very scientifically-minded expert in my office, and gave him a demonstration of centre of gravity in relation to bowling, and he was not only genuinely impressed, but remarked: 'That is the best and most convincing thing I have had put before me, and should settle all arguments as to how a player should hold his bowl.'

Another to whom I demonstrated was inclined to argue, until we came to a certain point. He said he could hold the bowl with the thumb half-way between the rings and the disc (his way), and still maintain centre of gravity. To that assertion I agreed, but what convinced him was this:—

While he could maintain centre in this manner, the bowl had to lie tilted in his hand, and anybody knows that a tilted bowl striking the green on the draw will produce a wobble, even if it is slight. You must deliver on the green with the centre of the bowl to get a straight, smooth run out of it.

By gripping it as I teach, and delivering it correctly, the very centre contacts the green, and it runs as cleanly and truly as if sent from a chute. Any tester who is not an amateur—and I don't agree that all licensed testers are experts—will tell you that without an eye to the centre of gravity he could not run the bowl down the table to the given marks as small as a sixpence denoted by the standard bowl. What is more convincing?

Many games are lost before they are begun. If you have

to meet an opponent with a reputation don't be afraid of him; respectfully scorn him.

One of the outstanding and necessary attributes in a soldier, a leader of men, or a successful bowler, is 'guts,' an understandable, if not a very elegant, wartime expression. One in every ten lacks it, yet could acquire it if he would.

Printed repetitions in these pages are merely variated reminders on important points or subjects; not fill-ups for spaces. Some subjects have many angles—the better for being kept separate.

The hand that rocks the cradle also sees to it that you are turned out to satisfaction. Remember, she's always:

> *Serving, saving, solving, soothing*
> *Round the clock from day to day;*
> *With a patient hand removing,*
> *All the briars from the way.*

BOWLS SMALL AND LARGE

THE average mind is liable to be greatly disturbed over the variety of opinions expressed concerning size of bowl needed.

Claims that the size decides the grip for any hand, irrespective of the fact that a wide range of sizes is offered, and other bogies, are constantly set out in press and club. These prompt some comment.

Wrote a well-known Australian champion of another equally known: 'He says a Size 6 ($5\frac{1}{16}$") bowl is worth five shots in 21 up over that of smaller sizes—Size 3 ($4\frac{7}{8}$") and Size 4 ($4\frac{15}{16}$")—and I agree with him.'

The author disagrees with both of them, while admitting that the larger and more weighty bowl has advantages—I play with a Size 7 ($5\frac{1}{8}$") 3 lb 7 oz (1560 grams) bowl. Reasons for disagreement are:

A small bowl can be pushed up by a large one much further than the reverse case. Admittedly, it can be pushed out further. Fast shots of all descriptions, however, can be more accurately played and greater speed attained, with the smaller sizes. Stick strictly to advice in earlier pages—20 and 21.

A big bowl will cut in the not-so-big, from all angles up

to jack high, and even beyond, when on the wing of a head. They are much easier to see, and hit, as well. Many claim that the minimum sizes have the points advantage. It is fifty-fifty.

A player, to do himself justice, should have two sets of bowls, to use as the occasion demands. Small bowls cut into a gale best. They are also preferable when the gale is behind them. Big bowls present a broader surface for the wind both ways. Outstanding play in my career was shown in New Zealand—a notoriously blowy area—with a Size 3 ($4\frac{7}{8}''$) bowl. Circumstances and conditions are the deciding factors.

The Henselite Bowls Company has supplied the following statistics, which speak for themselves:

Sales records shows that 10% use Size 0 ($4\frac{5}{8}''$), 12% the Size 1 ($4\frac{3}{4}''$), 12% the Size 2 ($4\frac{13}{16}''$), 17% the Size 3 ($4\frac{7}{8}''$), 23% the Size 4 ($4\frac{15}{16}''$), 21% the Size 5 ($5''$), 4% the Size 6 ($5\frac{1}{16}''$) and 1% the Size 7 ($5\frac{1}{8}''$).

WHAT IS A YARD-ON SHOT?

THE term is a clouded one at any time, and should be cut out of the average bowler's stock of knowledge as too elastic for common understanding, or acceptance. Let us take an end or two, and see how perplexing this instruction becomes, particularly to the younger generation.

You will hear a skip call to one of his men, when there is a bowl, say, a yard to the rear, or the end is a little congested: 'Give me a yard-on shot.' The unfortunate player, not desiring to establish his ignorance by seeking a more explicit direction, plays what he thinks is a 'yard-on' shot.

Then the skip protests: 'Oh, no, I didn't mean you to be strong.' If the player fails to reach the head, he will be just as likely to say: 'Oh, I wanted you to come up to it.' That last phrase gets the subordinate more perplexed than ever.

To 'come up to it' conveys to the average player about as much information as 'give me a yard through.' He could 'come up to' a head without running past it, yet that particular shot might be quite useless for the lie of the head at the moment.

So we must define what a 'yard on' really means. If skips

and thirds had an understanding about the various terms, less disagreements, even though they be friendly ones, would be recorded.

My advice is to drop the term 'yard-on' altogether, for it may mean 'put a yard on to your first,' or it may mean anything. If you want a head disturbed and your man to 'come up to it,' don't use either term, but something more understandable, such as: 'Come through with about a yard of green,' or a foot, or two feet, as the position demands.

Avoid using the term. To tell a man to 'put a yard on' is not only not understandable, but a common phrase with all skips. You might say: 'Just bend into the head with a foot of green,' or a yard, as the case may be, for conditions and other things have to be considered, and they can only be considered on the day of play and the lie of the head.

TO MAKE THE BOWL DO YOUR BIDDING

IT has been demonstrated on the testing table that when bowls strike any surface on a point other than their running line, or centre, the bias is affected. The 'balance test' reveals this to such an extent that all sorts of courses are taken, on the table, even by bowls being tested.

Similarly, a player can so affect the running of a bowl, up to the first 40 or 50 ft (12-15 m) as to delay the action of the bias. This is done by, first, holding the bowl as shown in Fig. 20, and then by grassing it while still on the 'cant.'

Both back and fore hands can be so treated. Only when the bowl adjusts itself, and begins to run on an even keel, will it regain its natural balance.

It may be asked: 'What is the object of canting and grassing, as described?' If there was no obstruction, or there wasn't 'a sleeper on the line,' it would have no value, of course.

But it is of very useful service when a short block, or even a three-quarter, is in the way. Together with other aids to defeating an obstruction, the latter should have no scares for the average player.

Of course, these bias-clipping antidotes only apply to getting inside, and not outside, a bowl in the running track. As in boxing, cricket, tennis, etc, footwork plays an essential and outstanding part. It returns us to the slogan once again, 'what you sow at the mat end, you reap at the jack end.'

I invariably cant my bowl for every kind of drive doing things to it that can only be achieved by experiment and long experience.

PLANTS, OR SET POSITIONS

WALKING up to view the head to note any alteration in the lie of it, is often necessary, and is a process not too popular with onlookers.

It becomes necessary because, in many cases, the marker is not competent to give an intelligent answer to some questions that might be asked, even when he is said to be competent, and the player has every right to think to the contrary, if he chooses. There are many lies that have to be viewed to discover their significance.

Not too many know what plants in billiards or bowls mean, and the scoring possibilities they present. They are many and varied, but just two are presented with these comments:

The first represents a head in a singles game. The jack lies eight inches ahead of the shot bowl, owned by the player with bowls marked X.

He needed two to win, in a game in which his opponent was 20. Walking up to see the lie, with his last bowl he played on to the opponent, lying behind his, the effect being to cut the jack across to two of his own, for game.

The second diagram demonstrates another lie, not often seen by the average player not accustomed to plants or set shots.

The player here needed three shots to win, and strolled up for a look. Why should he play blind when the rule allows him to view as often as he pleases?

By contacting the shortest bowl shown in the diagram with an 'up' shot, the bowl marked X contacts kitty, and jars it across to the right, to gain three shots required for game. It was one of the prettiest and brainiest shots I had witnessed of many examples of the plant variety.

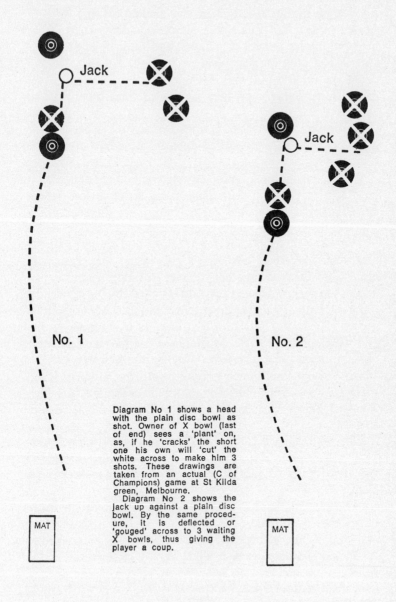

No. 1

No. 2

MAT

MAT

Diagram No 1 shows a head with the plain disc bowl as shot. Owner of X bowl (last of end) sees a 'plant' on, as, if he 'cracks' the short one his own will 'cut' the white across to make him 3 shots. These drawings are taken from an actual (C of Champions) game at St Kilda green, Melbourne.

Diagram No 2 shows the jack up against a plain disc bowl. By the same procedure, it is deflected or 'gouged' across to 3 waiting X bowls, thus giving the player a coup.

SOMETHING ABOUT DRIVING IN SINGLES

FROM time to time it is written and advised: 'Don't drive in singles games.' But this advice almost invariably comes from the non-driving writers or authors, and must be entirely disregarded, if only for that reason.

On the other hand, very seldom, if ever, does the known driver advise against practice, except to warn others not to become slaves to it.

Performing in fours, pairs, singles or any other department of the game, a player is called upon to bring into use all the shots generally known.

Whether it be fours, pairs, or singles, the proposition on a head has to be dealt with, and there is no logical reason why the performer should depart from a set shot because it happens to be singles play.

The lie of a head calls for the best and most profitable means of converting it to one's gain when the position is against. So that the urge not to drive in singles games is just so much nonsense. Good, timely drives often pay big dividends.

In any kind of game at bowls, 'play the shot as you see it' is a good slogan. For centuries 'skittling,' as it is termed in the Old World, was very little indulged in, the skittler being regarded with great disfavour. We live in a new age.

But visiting Englishmen have informed the author that old prejudices are dying fast, and must, in order that the high standard shown in Australia and New Zealand might be kept abreast.

Play your singles games, then, as you would play in any other competition. Happy is he, all the same, who has acquired the art of knowing just when to drive and when to leave it alone.

When the student has made good, reached the driving stage of his career, and subsequently attains to that high standard expected of him, he then becomes the best judge as to whether he should drive or leave it alone in any department of the game.

If there were only roses and no other kind of flower it would indeed be a drab world. If bowlers were all alike in temperament, ability and outlook it would be still more drab. Jones can't be Smith and Jones, too. Brown must remain distinct from Robinson. Treat and accept each from his particular angle, just as you expect to be viewed.

A BAD INVESTMENT

THE object of all that is contained in these pages lies in the instructive, and to that end let us visualise a game in progress. Two single-handed experts, a good green.

At some, or any stage of the game, one player decides to put in a short block. The other disdains any ideas of being forced on to the hand that is shut up, or to play too narrowly or too wide, and proceeds to make his effort.

Not one bowler in every 1000 practises the short (45 to 50 ft or 14-16 m) block. The few who are told the multitude who don't that it is a loser, a wasted bowl, no good, etc, etc.

These sentiments come from those who know nothing of, or have not exploited, the possibilities or science of protecting a head.

'Where does the lesson come in?' someone may ask. We must not allow ourselves to be prejudiced against anything we are either unable to accomplish or do not practise. Nobody ever applauds a short block that succeeds in keeping out an opponent's bowl. That is why psychology of the bank-seat remains an interesting subject.

It is a mistake not to acknowledge an approximately good effort. The tendency to show the onlookers that the obstruction is merely a guide is not a lucrative investment.

YOUR PRECIOUS EYESIGHT

GOOD eyesight is one of the most precious possessions of those fortunate enough to retain it. How long it can be retained, and to what age, depends upon the individual and how he or she treats it.

My own particular case will serve to demonstrate how good eyesight may be preserved, and the use of glasses, except for reading small print, unnecessary.

During my bowling career, and up to now, I have not used glasses except for reading, and am certain that many thousands of others would be in a position to testify similarly had they followed my set policy.

It is a duty to warn bowlers not to be in a great hurry to have their eyes tested, with a view of using glasses on the green. Few opticians will tell you, as one—an officer of a bowling association—told me: 'Put off the evil day.'

The casual observer sees on all sides the spectacle of 50 per cent of humanity saddled with defective vision.

Blessed is the bowler who can dispense with artificial assistance in his sport.

Following the course of opponent's bowls up the green continuously brings eyestrain as surely as night follows day. Make a point of not looking up until his bowl, in your judgment, is finishing its run.

Fasten your eyes on the ground at your feet or a flower bed. Following the course of opponent's bowls also brings nerves in its train, anticipating, as the player does, that something is going to happen.

Come up with your next bowl unruffled and calm, with a new vision after those seconds of rest for the eyes.

The time-honoured rolling is excellent treatment, which can be carried out while sitting in tram, train, or car, with lids closed. Opening the eyes under cold water and massaging the temples are most beneficial.

Avoid bad focus when attending pictures, and don't listen to urges to 'get glasses before your eyes are ruined.'

KEEP FIT DURING WINTER MONTHS

IT is quite a mistake for bowlers domiciled in states or countries where the greens have to be closed down for the winter to assume that they have necessarily to put themselves away in cotton-wool till the spring.

The greens in those places are all closed down, except for a few winter rinks here and there. Bowlers put their bowls away, and allow the next three or four months to unfit them for the new season. They lose their playing condition, and are minus the exercises to be derived from the game.

But why should any bowler play the role of Rip Van Winkle? I don't see any reason why the learner and the man who needs his daily exercise should not be active and continue to improve himself. The value of homework cannot be unduly stressed.

It will not only assist to mould you, but keep you healthy, and the exercise is the best in the world for the kidneys. Just do the work anywhere that is convenient; practise the grip, stance, and the delivery, both hands. Also the swinger, the drive, and the short step. Let your imagination have full-play. You need never let the bowl out of your hand in these exercises.

When not playing for four years, I did these exercises daily, kept fit, and, although not having put a bowl to grass, dropped right into my form. There is no imagination about this.

I would guarantee to make a good player of raw material with four weeks at home. So why not continue to mould yourself through the winter and be cherry ripe for the spring? I think a spell is beneficial, but this practice is so gentle, just sufficient to retain your touch, keeping your muscles hard and your bowls brain from rusting.

Though never before in the history of the game were prospective bowlers asked to begin their tuition at home, or given homework to do, until I pioneered it, I note with satisfaction that some other men competent to teach their fellows are emulating the move. One reason why the continent is cram-full of bad bowlers, contortionists, all impossible of improvement is because this modern idea was unknown, and new members were taken straight on to the green and well and truly spoilt.

Many players fail to strike form for some weeks after the vacations peculiar to those states or countries which have to close down their greens.

The man who has a bowl beside him at home, however, comes to hand at once, and suffers no physical or muscular inconvenience.

SIDESHOWS OF THE SPORTS

THE very best of good players will be beaten, at intervals, in any outdoor sport. Therefore, never feel depressed at defeat in bowls.

The consistent, dependable player, or side, will mostly win under good conditions, but anything may happen, as history records, under bad.

Critics, especially those not competent to criticise, will arise in attempts to pull you down. Don't be pulled down.

When viewing any game it is a good habit to focus on the effort, not the personality behind the effort.

Good playing conditions, eliminating tricky greens, should be kept in view constantly. All that is left for players defeated by inferior talent on bad greens—which covers much ground —is to take it with the best possible grace.

Mostly their excuses are based on things not apparent to the casual eye. We hear of rinks 'not playing,' and remarks such as 'I could not get it,' etc. Be sympathetic.

This levelling up of players is the cause of more defeats than is generally supposed. The Press report of matches, merely recording defeats, is no guide or explanation of many a tragedy.

A LESSON ON TIMING

SPLIT-SECOND timing is one of the first essentials for a successful career at bowls.

We have no need to be reminded that some succeed despite textbook recommendations, but their numbers are infinitesimal.

Writers who continue to point out that this, or the other player won any particular game without using the drive, or that he upset all textbook theories, one way or another, unconsciously advertise their own shortcomings.

Split-second timing and how to acquire it should be the subject of early study by the newcomer.

It is never too late (though perhaps difficult) to acquire it on the part of those some years in the game.

Teaching a person to time his actions indoors before he ever treads a green is only one of the prime reasons why my pupils have excelled everywhere.

At this point, I invite the reader to enter any club enclosure and check up on what he sees in the delivery department.

He will find that over 90 per cent of the players in all positions, protrude or thrust the left leg (right-handers) so prematurely, so as to upset all balance.

When they poise, they may be streamlined in everything, but with that fatal premature left-foot step, a square-on follow-through goes up in smoke. The powerful become no more powerful than those many stones less in weight.

To accomplish rhythmical, correct timing, which adds direction and control to its virtues, certain joints must be employed, on both sides of the body.

They are twelve in number, in conjunction with the spine.

Thus the player has twelve joints all closely related to timing, inasmuch as that all should be used in a split-second effort.

Not only control, but power, is acquired, and how much more stylish and rhythmical it looks.

To accomplish these movements, the improver should take a tennis ball into a carpeted room, lay a mat and practise the movements. He will soon find how much more powerful he has become.

He must never allow the left foot to move the slightest until the bowling arm is on the forward swing.

The result should be that the left foot just beats the hand holding the bowl by four to six inches, at the point of delivery.

A personal note is that this simultaneous use of those twelve joints over fifty years has kept me at thirty-five-forty, and will do so with you.

Possibly, with the greatest number, this is the most important consideration. A man is healthier using all his muscular development at once than loading some with the lot.

Most bowlers are human rocking horses, quarrelling with their own joints, muscles, sinews and general make-up by a follow-the-leader process out of step with the dictum that we play bowls primarily for exercise.

BOWLING TO INCHES

IN all calculations relating to bowling, we must assume that we are playing on true surfaces, under good conditions. Playing a rink that is not true is quite another thing.

Be careful that the mat is always square-on with the rink as this is important, being the base upon which the position of the feet is determined. The player on, say, No 4 rink stands with his shoulders squarely facing the boundary peg between 4 and 5 rinks. He holds the bowl so that it rests at the estimated position for the correct elevation and points directly at the peg.

That is the player's 'line' and lines contribute a very important part in all things appertaining to bowls. His feet are in their accustomed place from which he estimates the length of step required to suit the pace of the green.

It is essential that the accustomed place be strictly adhered to; haphazard standing is to be avoided if consistency is desired. If regarded from a mathematically calculated angle, then exactitude must appeal. Once more 'what you sow at the mat end, you reap at the jack end.' The same careful standing applies equally to a back hand shot, only the aiming point will be the boundary peg between 3 and 4 rinks.

The selection of the length and position of the first step will determine the final position of the bowl at the head. Having observed the result and assuming that the player has put into practice all the combinations that have been taught, then if a correction be necessary it becomes a function of the player's intelligence. However, once a satisfactory result is obtained, then an exact repetition will enable the player to literally bowl to inches.

A LAW UNTO THEMSELVES

WHILE nobody can claim monopoly to propound methods on how the game should be approached, and played, the man with a limited degree of success is always dangerous to the incomer.

After gaining a title, he is invited, or invites himself, to contribute to general knowledge. He might be successful in his play on quite good lines, but mostly such is not the case, and this is where caution is needed.

Many of these well-meaning, come-and-go exponents, insist that driving in singles does not pay, that the comfortable grip is the correct grip, that as the bowl is taking the back swing, the left foot should step out, etc, etc.

The bulk of highly successful players describe their methods without advocating them, and this is a correct attitude, for 90 per cent have some failings that, if acquired by others, would be fatal to the latters' career.

THE BEST FAIL SOMETIMES

EVERY defeated player has the privilege of seeking for the cause of his downfall, at any time, or in any match. When he does, it is usually said of him that he is looking for a way out. While the latter course is by no means the most unpopular, great men in the game have been shown to have been more than justified.

Generalities make positions obscure, but history is an infallible guide. An exponent who could be included in Australia's best half-dozen, over all time, once had a 'cricket score' compiled against him in a singles classic.

Then somebody defeated his vanquisher some hours after, on another green, with another cricket score, yet grades below the first-beaten in class.

'Clean slates' are among the records as numerous as pancake days. It does not follow that all these figures relate solely to bad or unplayable conditions. Hundreds of others could be quoted, and most are due to pure, unaccountable lapses.

This or that champion is not necessarily done, or on his last legs, because of temporary lapses, or being made to look foolish in certain circumstances that occur, and will continue to occur, while the game is played.

After one of these debacles, the author said to a 33–3 defeated man: 'Don't lose any sleep over that; you are still the great player we know you to be,' etc. 'I will feel the sting much less for you having said that to me,' he replied, looking quite cheered up. It is consistency that counts in bowls, not a loss or a victory, one way or the other.

Every man of pretension—including myself—has been made to look foolish on the day by prevailing conditions. Only the Juggins who sit round and not even play well with their remarks, talk same for one as the other. In a gale the players are fellows in misfortune, neither losing prestige by defeat.

A champion player-writer announced in his own column: 'I have evolved something that enables me to hit a bare jack anything from 5 to 11 times in succession.' Right on top of that declaration, he was in need of a single point, his opponent wanting 11 for game.

For more than an hour there were 'bare jacks' offering, but

none was hit, and the 13 points compiled made him a loser. The man was never born who could hit up to 11 bare jacks except as an occasional freak demonstration.

I am not satisfied that a man has slipped or is not as good as he used to be until I see him beaten consistently under conditions that call for no alibis. Selectors, in particular, should not take notice of known expert players being defeated on surfaces that level-up all and sundry. Despite occasional tragedies to themselves of the order described, the expert player knows his true form and what he can do. Consistency is the key that opens the door to values; lapses come, and go with the wind.

PLAY THE BIG HAND WHEN ALTERATION IS VITAL

IMAGINE yourself the player who has to disturb a vital end, or lose a match. The opponent is lying 'game,' and something has to be done. In other departments of bowls, of course, the same position constantly arises.

Now look at Diagram 1, and then at Diagram 2.
They represent (1) the big proposition to bring about an alteration, and (2) the very much slenderer position.

Playing on the fore hand to the big lie of the head, the chance of contact is very much greater than if the back hand was chosen. Why?

On the fore hand there are no ports, or entrances, to go through, without taking either bowls or jack in the run. What also makes that hand big is the fact that there are 32 inches points of contact.

Add to that the best part of another four or five inches, the size of the bowl you are using, to contact outer portions, and you have a target of approximately 40 in (100 cm).

Turn, now, to the same lie reversed. Many players make the mistake of taking the hand that allows the bowl used to pass through comparatively big spaces, on either side of the jack, thus losing any chance of getting at least another end.

The lesson taught per medium of these drawings refers, of course, mostly to games where, if an alteration is not made, the match is lost. In such cases, therefore, always look for, and play, the big hand.

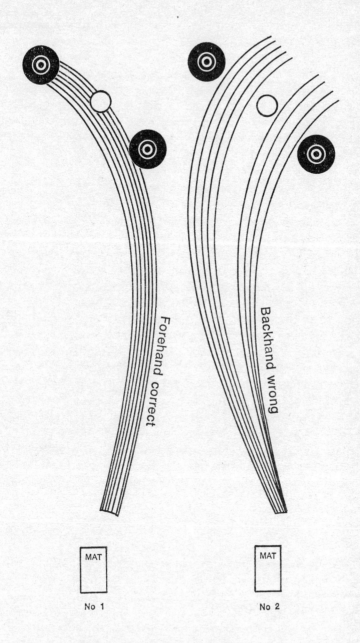

Forehand correct

Backhand wrong

MAT
No 1

MAT
No 2

Should a novice enter for competitions out of his class? Definitely yes! My first essay being a State singles championship, what other answer could I give to this important, and often-asked question? That initial essay being a successful one, another angle presents itself. What one can perform, another can also accomplish. Defeats in a bowler's early career fit him for standing up to the hard games when he becomes seasoned. Immediate success comes to few, and at times is a flash in the pan. It all depends upon whether a correct foundation is laid.

OUT OF CONTROL

A PLAYER is out of control when he fails to adjust the length of his step to the swing of his arm for the varying distances being played. He is in effect off balance.

Yet on any green on any day we can see players constantly stepping the same length. Which might be quite all right as long as the surface is not keen, say, more than 12 sec.

Many individual games are on record as lost on account of this defect in a player's outfit, and some have been outstanding.

In a famous match between two equally famous players, one man won so easily that it was described in the vernacular as 'no game!' Why? The green was particularly fast (17-19 sec), and one limited his step to about nine to twelve inches. He was in control.

It was observed that he increased his step and therefore his swing as the lengths increased. The other adopted a constant length step, and was always strong on the short lengths.

Had the two met on a slow green the game may not have been one-sided, because the loser would not have been out of control.

Out of control. The term looms large in modern bowling. And you will often lose control on fast surfaces if you don't regulate the step to suit the length thrown.

In the 'know your man' connection, always give an opponent a short to medium length if you find he is a one-spot stepper, when the green is fast—particularly when it is extra fast (19-20 sec).

The one-length steppers should benefit by the lesson and practise the shorter movements. It means many points difference. The teaching applies to all departments—singles, fours and pairs.

During his long connection with the game the author has been surprised at the small number of players who take advantage of this simple method of controlling length.

HARD WAY THE BEST

COACHES of the present, as in the past, will always find their students, if correctly taught, respond to such teaching.

But when given a position in a good team, or contesting singles games, they fade out and disappoint themselves and their mentors. Why?

The reason is best explained through my personal experience when entering the game, an experience only too common today.

A personal study with visits to several greens convinced me that there was nobody worth emulating, so decided to teach myself over several months.

First entry was for the Singles Championship of the State, which I subsequently won and went on to take all the classics.

But where encouragement was expected, only ridicule and cheap mirth provoking abuse came, and I was told: 'Don't make a fool of yourself and the club.'

But little did the ridiculers forsee that they were prescribing a tonic of incalculable value, not only for me, but posterity.

That ridicule and want of encouragement (I was in the early thirties) stung, but implanted a feeling of determination to maintain confidence in myself, and 'show 'em,' as it were.

It is a mistake to spare your pupils. To one in whom I had great hopes, I said after he had shown the white feather: 'Fancy *you* falling down on your courage.'

It was a head in a singles as big as a wash tub, with four shots on a short end and making faces at the soldier pupil.

The colour mounting to his temples displayed the effect that bit of bluff had on his morale, just as those of my clubmates had upon me.

But it paid dividends, for that chap took the bit and became one of the best players in his time.

It is often cruel to be kind, but you have to make them ashamed of any tendency towards the inferiority complex.

In the case of this chap, who had allowed the four points to be built because he had developed the temporary jitters at the prospect of losing a full hand, I said at the end of the game: 'I will set that head up and will ask you to deal with it as you have been taught.' I got tired of setting it up afresh, as he never failed again.

Without the spirit: 'It's never lost till it's won,' all the skill in rolls up is useless. It must be a routine habit.

In giving advice on how to play any particular game, a writer must necessarily throw modesty to the four winds.

When I entered the game, and had a look round at a multiplicity of performers, none not merely did not impress, but left the notion that none could be copied.

Elsewhere, I have stressed the important point of not being carried away by someone's success. Keep that in mind.

It has been publicised that the greatest of all teachers (Marchesi) could not sing a note. By the same rule, there were many at that period who thrilled everyone, but could not teach a note satisfactorily.

But these references cannot be applied to a game. I have frequently written that success in the field must precede the attempt to tell others how. Even many of our top-liners are something to avoid.

TEMPERAMENT

IT is an accepted fact that in all sport temperament plays a leading part, but very often the term is misplaced and made use of in order to offset other characteristics peculiar to the individual, not altogether in his favour.

What man is not temperamental, more or less? And, after all, who is going to be the judge as to what particular brand of the temperamental species is for good or bad in anyone? A temperamental person is one who shoots little sparks of electricity from unexpected parts, illuminating the imagination of his critics. The modern dictionary tells us that it is 'disposition.' So that a man with a vicious disposition will act viciously, and a man with a timid disposition, or one with not much confidence in himself, will act timidly or without confidence.

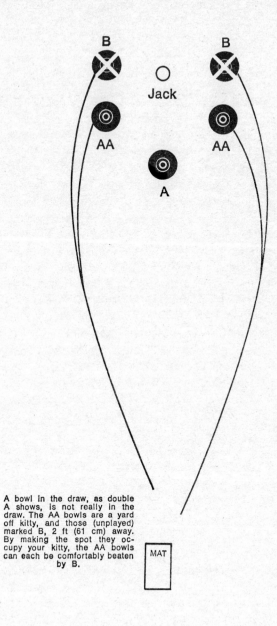

B

B

Jack

AA

AA

A

A bowl in the draw, as double A shows, is not really in the draw. The AA bowls are a yard off kitty, and those (unplayed) marked B, 2 ft (61 cm) away. By making the spot they occupy your kitty, the AA bowls can each be comfortably beaten by B.

MAT

Men have been repeatedly chosen for high positions owing to their alleged correct temperament, but lacking in the ability to back it up by their play. There are various brands of temperament—the fighting or determined species, the inferiority complex assortment, the nervous, irritating and mannerish kinds, also the suspicious, self-conscious variety. We see these in all their glory everywhere the game is played.

My experience is that the alleged temperamentals invariably make the best players in all sport; in fact, most leading sportsmen we know are highly strung.

I would plump for the man with the fighting spirit whose outstanding characteristic is: 'Yes, I can do the job!' This trait is sufficient to cover a multitude of weaknesses.

The ideal man, of course, is he who possesses the ability, plus the fighting characteristic, plus the will to take the bad with the good. Those with undue strain are impossible. Many good players show a tendency at some period of their career to develop the jumps, and one to whom I pointed this out, assuring him that he would beat it sooner or later, felt aggrieved.

'What is the matter with me? I get well into things, only to fade out near the finals.' That question was asked me by one who subsequently overcame it. 'If you won't be offended, I will tell you.' He replied with a smile: 'Carry on.' 'Well, you want to get that heart of yours removed from the vicinity of your socks up to the region of your waistcoat.' And he did. A great player later.

No man ever reached such a stage of advancement that someone could not tell him of a weakness not apparent to himself. In accepting the dictum, that player defeated his weakness, and was obliged for being told.

CHOOSING A CHAMPION FOUR

FOR all time there have been discussions and expressions of opinion on the question of the best method to adopt in forming a champion four in big games. Perhaps I am in a good position to give a little advice on this all-important matter.

In selecting a four a skipper has to be guided by certain features. In the first place, he must be sure that he, and not anybody else, will lead or run the four. In this respect it is usually wise to steer clear of another skip as third man.

The second man should be chosen from the ranks of second men, and not third men. The former are usually quiet customers, who know their job, but having opinions, keep them to themselves. Third men, playing as seconds, frequently upset everybody and everything around them by their expressions as to what the skip should or should not play or have played.

Men of quiet demeanour who don't want to argue the point are preferable.

You only have to look at some of the alleged champion combinations, as formed, to conclude that inexperience in placing the units is the outstanding weakness. Nothing is worse, nothing more undoing, and nothing tends less to success than the loquacious, know-all, voice-raising third man.

In selecting him, choose one who will tell you of any alteration, but otherwise be silent; take the bad with calm and sympathy, and the good with eulogy fitting the particular occasion or shot.

Two points only need be seriously considered in choosing a second man. The first and paramount is his draw shot ability. It must be of a high standard. If he has a nice up shot he is most useful, and you are fortunate in your choice. The third-second who wants to drive or play into the head repeatedly should be kept at arm's length.

The leader should be strictly a leader. Take the man who specialises in the job, and who can throw the kitty well. You need look for nothing else outside of one essential, and that applies to all four. This last point must not be allowed to escape you in the choice.

No matter how good a player any man may be locally, he must stand up to the job in big games. One who gets nippy, or who cannot be spoken to without becoming upset, is no good to any four. Choose men who don't get jittery and who are prepared to concentrate wholly on their particular job, and they will beat all the fancy fours.

Before you choose at all for a classic or a big tournament, look yourself well over. Are you good enough? I don't mean to infer that anybody has a right or monopoly to these things, but rather that burlesquing the game is not good for it.

I see many, many skips in big events who ought to be purely onlookers, men who can't drive and are not versatile. I see them playing over third men who are superior in every way to themselves. I see them wholly lacking in generalship, strategy and personality, plus experience. Don't skip unless you can.

LEADER, SECOND, THIRD AND SKIP

THE LEADER

To sum up the leader in a rink game, you have to show what his duties are, and how he should carry them out, together with the things that he must avoid. The very first thing that the layer of the mat should do is to have a preliminary talk with his skip on the question of general policy, for he should be ever mindful of the important fact that he is subordinate to the skip's wishes, and not run away with the mistaken idea that he can throw the kitty where he likes, and play and bowl on either hand.

That being understood, he should see that the mats at each end are in order, the length quite whole and fit to play off. When he lays the mat he should see that the point of the take-off, i.e., where the bowls will make contact with the green, is smooth, and the best he can pick, having regard to both hands.

This is important from the fact that when a bowl strikes the green and lands in a dent, a corrugated or rough spot, the spin or turn given to it by the fingers is nullified, sometimes to the extent of many feet. Then, in trying to beat it, the player goes flying to the other extreme past the head. A smooth take-off means bowls round the kitty; a rough one might mean anything. You may correct a bad bowl on a smooth take-off, but it becomes a gamble from the rough.

The leader, especially if he has had some prior practice on the rink, should speedily adopt a policy. That is to say, he should settle down to the good 'playing' hand, and not keep chopping about. If the fore is the good hand, play it. If the opponent drops short on the good hand, don't be driven to the bad. Play as though it was not there.

Don't throw the jack anywhere, but inches from where the skip indicates. If you can't throw it to about 5 ft (1.5 m) your education is not complete. If it so happens that you have a preference—don't deceive yourself, as 75 per cent have—play the preference hand for all you are worth, if it is a good hand. If it's the bad hand, throw preference overboard.

There is very little else a leader has to think about; good take-off, consistent jack throwing at all lengths, playing the good hand, even if the opponent is in the way (with few exceptions)—showing discretion, of course, if lying the shot on that hand, and a danger of turning an opponent in with the second bowl.

What should a leader avoid? There are quite a number of things. He should particularly avoid giving his side many varying lengths, throwing them all over the place. When the length has to be changed, the leader must take his cue from the skip. He should avoid twisting, by which is meant this: A leader has been playing a hand to perfection, and then, for some unaccountable reason, he endeavours to show that he can play the other just as well. Don't do it!

Also don't 'put one at the back' if the first is a good, close one. Make them both close—touchers every time, if you can. On no account try to run the opponent off the kitty or the head down to your own first bad one.

A leader's mission is round the kitty; sooner or later, if not the actual shot, but reasonably close, even though beaten with both bowls, yours has a splendid chance of being turned in, but if you have a go, and attempt to trail the kitty away, you give the No 2 the same right to play 'perhapsers,' and the skip arrives at the end so many down, and nothing to work on. Think that term out—what 'work on' means— for three players come after you, looking for something to work on. Therefore, lay the foundation for them.

There is little else for a leader to study beyond these few simple rules, and the most important of the lot is to keep on drawing round that kitty, leaving the pushing out and the 'trailing to' to the others. A good leader is like a foundation to a house, good or bad, and spelling stability, or the other thing. Those who specialise in the job should practise kitty-throwing at all lengths.

NUMBER TWO

All places in a good four have their values; all are contributors to the common end, and the common end is to get one to eight bowls closer to the kitty than the other side, and retain them. To do this the leader, the second, third and skip must throw individuality to the four winds and work as a team. No 2 may suggest, but not demand, anything relative to measuring.

No 2's duty (we can dispense with the formalities, such as filling the card, putting the scores up, etc) is to stand right behind the leader, and 'get' the green, knowing just the difference in the 'take' of his own bowls (if any) to the leader's.

One of the first things a second man must get into his head, and keep there, is that if the leader is strong, and the other leader close to kitty, he must immediately appoint himself a second leader, and not try running the kitty. This fatal error is most common with a second man. A shrewd skip will not ask for or permit it, but get his No 2 to concentrate on beating the leader, or giving the third man and himself something to work on.

The actual duties of a second man are so few that they can be dismissed. All know that they must keep the card correctly, post the scores without fail every second end, and follow other simple formalities. The real value of a No 2 lies in what he must do and avoid in the play, and we will concentrate on that.

He must not urge the leader to something he favours, but leave him entirely in the hands of the skip—that would not be team work if he did. Of all things, No 2 must be 'up,' for if he is short he blocks the third man, and disaster sets in. At the same time, don't overdo the 'be-up' policy, for, when the leader fails, finessing with the third man by the skip becomes impossible if the No 2 also runs too far beyond the head.

I take the view that a second man can be forgiven more than a leader when playing short, for he tries hard not to over-run, and sometimes drops short for that reason. Never 'take the bit'; it spells lots of bad things, and is not team work. Taking the bit means playing a shot not asked for by the skip. Obey to the letter.

Study the changes of length, play the good hand whenever the skip gives you preference, and especially if it is your preference hand. Don't ask or look for a drive; things are desperate when the skip calls for one. Keep on drawing, for the dead-draw No 2 is the winner of matches. Every classic I have won, outside of singles, has pointed to the No 2's success. That is why I declare for the best draw No 2 in big games.

The No 2 should not get behind the third man and signal to the skip. Sometimes it causes him to play the wrong shot. A third signalling one second shot and the No 2 two second shots causes the skip to drive and when disaster comes he says: 'Joe signalled that we had two seconds, so I took the risk.' No 3 correctly replied: 'Joe has no right to signal anything.'

NUMBER THREE

No 3 has his rights as a conversationalist; the two preceding him have not. No 3 can argue, make his views known, but cannot force them. If he is ignored, he should go quietly. Many third men turn to the bank and grumble, or tell the selector, or selectors, that 'he won't take my directions.' One or the other must be wrong: if it is the skip, then he should change places with the third, who 'knows better.'

Duties of third man—what are they?

One is not to give any direction whatever, unless the head has been disturbed, or there is something that has escaped the skip. The most successful combinations are the silent ones. A talking third man is a tragedy, a discreet and silent one a treasure. The first duty of a No 3 is to see that the leader does not place the mat in the rough with a bad take-off. This much neglected duty means points for or against a side.

Immediately the leader starts off, the third man should, with No 2, stand in the rear and 'get' the green. He should not urge either of the other players to do something contrary to the directions of the skip. The one and great thing a third man should padlock himself to is to get that saving shot for the side.

That means restraint. Don't gamble at bowls: play the Scotch game, and when things are looking bad on the head concentrate on getting that invaluable saver for the skip. It is all very well to say in the mind of a third man: 'If I miss it he'll get it.' That is bad politics; it is the duty of No 3 to produce that saver, which means safety first.

It is not the role of third man to collect the skip's bowls, as so often written—it is a nice courtesy, and entirely in the hands of the individual. Many do it, many do not, but having to collect and clean a bowl often spoils a skip's concentration, and brings him in contact with someone who would have a little talk with him before he takes the mat.

Third men should do all at their end that a skip cannot do at his. See that the other two do not develop wanderlust, make understandings known that are not understood, and generally keep an eye to the smooth running of the game. One point I would stress: Don't 'fight' the skip, or force views that are contrary to his. He has built up the head, and even if there are eight against him, and he knows it and plays any kind of a shot not in keeping with the views of the other three, no-body has a right to prevent him. Cross-purposes reflect themselves in the scores, and if the season finishes disastrously for a four the remedy lies in the removal of the skip.

THE CAPTAIN

Everybody knows the ideal captain, and everybody knows the other species, that range from good to very bad. The duties of a skip are also known, and it would be so much waste of space to go over all we read from time to time about 'don't irritate your men,' or 'don't drive when there are so-and-so against you,' or 'don't leave the land open for the enemy,' and such-like pleasantries.

A skip's success or failure will reflect itself in the results. I will lay down that a skip must be 'the goods'; must have all the shots, and be able to satisfy the selectors, before he is chosen, that he possesses all the attributes expected of him. He does not want lessons in etiquette, for if he neglects the usual principles he fails, and knows it.

The first attribute I would ask for in choosing a captain

would be that he must fill the bill as a player; other things being very secondary to that. The coaxing skip is no use unless he has all the shots and is efficient. His aim should be results; if he gets them he is in, if he fails he is out, all things being equal with his team. A good 'old' skip who retains his physical condition is only 'done' in the eyes of those who covet his job.

ARE YOU A PINCHER?

IF every bowler answered this question correctly, it would be found that 75 out of every 100 would reply, 'Possibly I am.' And that is so. There is more energy, more futile effort, and more golden opportunities lost through players pinching their bowls on the back hand than could be imagined.

It takes some courage for a man to acknowledge that he is a pincher, but nobody knows it better than his skipper. Of course, quite a percentage of skips do the same thing. It has been said that the onlooker sees most of the game, and in this connection he certainly does.

I have seen men play one bowl after another, although constantly reminded of it, narrow, narrow, narrow. It often occurs that a player gets nippy, or up on his toes, if told about it, which he should not.

What is the explanation, and why such an army? And, again, why don't they realise the fault? Let us take the queries separately. The explanation is that many players don't face in the direction they are going to bowl, and have a sort of side-on stance.

After a man has been standing wrongly, facing wrongly, for a long period, it is very difficult to break him. He is set and almost past redemption. But I will never be persuaded that any intelligent being cannot get away, with a little perseverance, from the bad habit of playing narrowly owing to not facing in the direction of the track his bowl must run over.

Many players do remedy the weakness, but, if not watched, will get right back to the old order, throw up their arms in disgust as the bowl takes a thin course up the green.

Using a bowl too large for the hand in order to get the weight, is neither clever nor commendable. More classics

125

have been won by the middle sizes down than otherwise. Sticking to the size of bowl a study of Fig. 2 gives you, is safe procedure, and shorn of bank-seat speculation. Having decided on the correct size of bowl to suit your hand, it is now possible to obtain the extra weight, if so desired, in any size.

GETTING THE BEST OUT OF MEN

A COMMON expression is often heard: 'He gets the best out of his men,' and this refers to different men in charge of, or skipping, fours in important matches. That certain skips do get better results is true, but it has to be there to get.

It is a very desirable quality, and one that is necessary in a leader of men, if he would be highly successful. Whether a man gets the best may be gauged from results, for that, all things being equal (if he has efficient players under him), is an infallible guide.

But I am afraid this generality, which some selectors are very fond of using, is much misunderstood, and not the least by themselves. I am referring to club selectors. Just analyse for a moment what getting the best out of your men amounts to.

It is said that a skip need only be very ordinary himself and yet get better results, which must mean figures, than another obtains, although the latter may be much superior. Just so much nonsense.

Let us take one with a coaxing, even please-everybody, temperament. We grant that these attributes are very fine and very desirable. He is admitted to be inferior to others, but on account of these good qualities is given the preference. For social games, very good; for competitive games, no!

If a player with a nicely balanced temperament hasn't the knowledge, he can't get the best, for his instructions are faulty.

At any particular end or part of a game, an instruction not given so that the maximum of gain be obtained, or is possible of attainment, so often witnessed from the bank, is not getting the best out of your men. It is only getting the best according to the lights of the instructor.

A very nice, even-tempered coaxing skip, and one not so splendidly equipped, may be confronted with precisely the same proposition in separate rinks. One may get a point out of the end, the other several points.

Now, if that kind so often pointed to as 'getting the best,' is minus the knowledge, hasn't the experience or the execution, he can't impart it to his men. A celebrated Australian skip used to have his men all trembling like aspen leaves, but he got the last ounce out of them by transferring his knowledge to them when giving instruction.

One must admit, however, that when the two combine—great knowledge and experience, with even temperament and coaxing ways, etc—the combination is 100 per cent good.

Temperamental players, the nervous easily-upset type, that have to be continually coaxed to get anything out of, are not much good under fire. Getting the best out of them is like telling a youngster that castor oil is just lovely. He doesn't fall for it; neither does the temperamental.

MORE ABOUT DRIVING

JUST as long as there are players who don't drive, because they have never acquired the art, so there will be columns printed at the instigation of these people in a futile endeavour to prove that it does not pay.

At the moment, a prominent personality, who is just an ordinary stock bowler, writes: 'I have played the game for fifty years, and say emphatically, that driving is not a paying proposition.' He does not even add: 'In reason,' but goes bald-headed for its elimination.

There are many such. If they lived to play for five hundred and fifty years, they would not make it pay, for the simple reason that it is not included in their repertoire.

One of the most prolific classic winners was asked by a pressman: 'What do you attribute your great success to: there must be a story behind it?'

'There is,' replied the other. 'Shortly, it is this: My opponent first has to beat me to the draw. Many have and many more will continue to do so, on the day. But when they do, they have to hold them, and the closer they pack their bowls, the worse they fare.'

Asked what he meant by 'pack,' the answer was: 'In

bowls, you must have an antidote, a Roland for the other fellow's Oliver. A drive of the deadly, devastating species, possesses, and rightly exploits, that antidote to the fullest advantage.'

When it is pointed out that certain lies on the green (and they are legion) cannot be reached except per medium of the fast drive, there is no answer, except that the drive has to be used.

Modern bowling, to be attractive, must retain that modicum of speculation which appeals to both players and onlookers. Reduce it to the drab and monotonous draw, draw, and good-bye to its popularity.

'I prefer a firm shot to driving,' is a remark often heard. Such people have only the firm shot, otherwise they would not make such an observation. There are innumerable positions that the firm or even much firmer shots cannot reach.

On one occasion, a non-driver, one who had repeatedly condemned the fast shots, was lying four and 'game' in a club singles. His opponent had one bowl to go. Stepping on to the bank, the former whispered to a friend: 'I only hope he doesn't drive.' The opponent did, took the jack through, and scored.

Need any more be said, or written? Perhaps just this: These good, anti-drive souls will always be with us, their slogan apparently embracing, 'What I can't do, you must not attempt or advocate.'

WEIGHT THE DECIDER

IN all drawing propositions the player should make himself as near to a human chute as is humanly possible, and never lose sight of the fact that, other movements being in keeping, the weight does it.

Bowls, played on scientific lines, or 'to figures,' plus 'the weight does it,' becomes just a question of calculation. Applying the correct elevation to the three different distances, the lowest laid bowl would run to the 66 ft (20 m) jack. The middle bowl would run to the 87 ft (26.5 m) jack, and the topmost to 108 ft (33 m). The human arm does not possess the machine accuracy of the chute, but it can be so approxi-

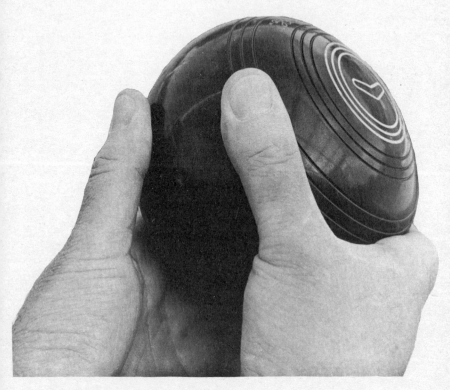

Fig. 20—The swerve drive to avoid contact with a block can only be acquired by intensive practice, and is not 'taught' in the pages of this treatise, on account of its complicated character. Often interrogated as to how the shot is accomplished, an illustration of the freak grip necessary to take all bias off the bowl is shown. A loose hold at first, gradually tightening to the point of delivery. Actually, the bowl being grassed on a cant, or slant, speed and bias engage in a 'fight', until the bias comes into its own well up towards the head, accounting for the swerve. Students should leave this department alone for a few seasons.

mate as to become extremely deadly and consistent. The above measurements, plus six feet at each end, provide the 120-ft (36.5 m) standard green.

WHEN IS A BOWL JACK HIGH?

QUESTIONS are asked with a view of safety, or danger. Any one of 1, 2, or 3 bowls contacted at several parts, particularly the left side, would often give unanticipated and disastrous results. If any such bowl is past or beyond the white, the danger is not there, hence necessity for accurate replies by markers. Terms don't always describe positions correctly. In the diagrams below, imagine the mat at the bottom of the page and to be bowling to the top of the page.

1. 1 This bowl is not jack high
       (Can be referred to as 'Short of jack high')

2. 2 This bowl is not jack high
       (Can be referred to as 'Short of jack high')

3. 3 This bowl is jack high

4. 4 This bowl is jack high
       (Can be referred to as 'Past jack high')

5. 5 This bowl is jack high
       (Can be referred to as 'Past jack high')

WELL-BUILT HEADS AND HOW TO DESTROY THEM

SINCE the third edition of this book was printed and circulated, the author has received many enquiries concerning an even more advanced and destructive method of nullifying heads built up by our friends 'the enemy,' otherwise our opponents.

While the third edition dealt with timing, as it is applied

to the drive, later experiments have had the effect of making this counter to well-built heads and dreams of holding them by the builder, dreams of despair.

According to your height, so you must shape your effort. It is only reasonable to assume that if a player can use all his limbs in conjunction, and simultaneously, the effort must produce a rhythmical and well-controlled effect.

In the following lesson you must bring your mathematical mind and imagination into play.

The player is set the problem of taking the jack through to the ditch from a head to which there is only a very narrow passage, or port, and which also necessitates taking all the bias off the bowl.

This can readily be accomplished by perfect timing, split second spinning, and release of the bowl, aided by the simultaneous movements of the various limbs: legs, arms, spine, knees, sinews, all contributing in that one effort that spells discomfort to the all-draw exponents of the game.

The player takes up his position, with soles of feet close up against the right-hand side. The demonstrator is 5 ft 8 in in height (1.7 m) and his timed stride for a fast drive is 4 ft (1.2 m) to a fraction of an inch—or a few millimetres—others in proportion to height.

The bowl is held at an elevation level with the chest, and when it is brought back behind the player it comes 2 ft 6 in (76 cm) to the rear of his feet. When it is subsequently swung, and the player's actions synchronise with the swing, the bowl is grassed, with perfect rhythm, 2 ft 6 in (76 cm) in front of the left foot, in line with the object.

This, then, produces a timed 9 ft (3 m) swing. For men of less height and those of greater height, the swing would be in proportion. Some 8 ft 6 in (2.5 m) and 9 ft 6 in (3 m) is a fair calculation.

The player stands with bowl poised, elevated level with the proposed step. Then it is brought back to that 2 ft 6 in (76 cm) behind. Later, when the stride has been accomplished and the bowl grassed—4 ft (1.2 m) stride, plus 2 ft 6 in (76 cm) at rear and same at front of the left foot.

It must be kept always in mind that in order to bring about the desired results, the step forward by the left leg must not

131

be made until the bowl is at the extreme distance—2 ft 6 in (76 cm) behind the player. Then, and only then, does he accomplish the 'go with' act that makes for balance, control, and direction. The physically weakest individual can get these actions, and a fast shot, if he studies and practises the movements.

Spin, which puts life in the bowl, is applied at the extreme termination of the swing, just as it is being grassed.

The whole action or movement might be likened to a comet, thin at one end and gradually becoming thicker. In other words, the effort should have a slow beginning and the pace gradually applied until the maximum is reached. Don't break your swing, keep the arm moving, slowly till furthest point at rear, then increasing as the forward step is made.

FURTHER POINTS ON DELIVERY

WHEN someone tells you the thumb on top is wrong, have a look at the grip the would-change-you artist adopts. Almost invariably he goes to the disc side of the ring.

Delivery is a product for good or evil omen. A wrong grip of the bowl, plus a too-lengthy step, on a fast green (14-16 sec) must produce a faulty, uncontrolled delivery.

A bowl gripped correctly, but grassed too far in front of the forward foot—some throw it as much as a yard at times—has a bad effect upon the delivery, causing the bowl to lose life.

Running and firm shots and fast drives must be of the 'daisy-cutter' variety to be effective. They cannot be that if the necessary contributory agencies are not there to bring them about.

Good or bad delivery, in short, is what you make it. It is the culminating point or terminus of the fundamentals you have been educated up to, or have educated yourself up to.

Standardisation of the fundamentals, or movements, as laid down in the earlier pages, present the would-be champion with a delivery that is in keeping with such movements, ensuring that same thing with each bowl regularity under all conditions.

A LESSON IN TACTICS

FOLLOWING upon a final game for one of Australia's biggest singles titles, a car-load of enthusiasts, including pressmen of the leading daily papers, discussed the pros and cons of the match. One particular incident caused the majority to agree on one point, viz, that a player should get the shot before getting position.

That view, however, is erroneous. In certain circumstances, or lies, it is excellent strategy to obtain position first. Here is one: The semi-final of a State Singles was being fought out, and the scores were 20-all in a 21-up game.

On an approximate 66 ft (20 m) length, the winner of the last head placed his first bowl square on the jack, the latter facing direct on to the rink number, the mat being six feet from rear ditch.

That, to the versatile player (and the other was distinctly so), was actually something in his favour, and the odds 6 to 4 against his opponent. This sounds optimistic, but why not? Had the opponent placed his first bowl—or even two, if the first was not good enough—down near the ditch in line, or approximately, with the number peg, he would have been in the best position.

Instead, he drew with his first two (both of which were short). He drove with his third and connected, but by this time his more astute opponent had secured a bowl three feet from the ditch, and another slightly further back.

Had the loser used his first bowl to obtain position, he had three left with which to force the jack down to it. Would not any moderate have sufficient confidence in himself to 'crack' the shot bowl with one of the three remaining?

Here is another case: The jack was on the six feet mark, and A side in fours championship lay shot, nine inches short. The B number two placed his first bowl in a direct line, behind it, and touching.

Skip B wanted two to win the match, and directed the next three bowls to 'as near the ditch [at right, the shot bowls not being quite square on to kitty] as you can get them.'

Of course it takes some courage to do these things, and

133

failure invariably brings repercussions, but nevertheless we don't look to first-class players to weaken on their courage, but rather to bank on their skill, as aforesaid. In many other lies it is by no means correct to say that the shot must be got before position is secured. The generality is an outer on the tactics target.

THE ROLE OF MARKER

A MARKER is merely a convenience to tell players the position at the jack end, and so save much time. In no sense is he an umpire. He cannot order contestants to do anything.

He is not in charge of the game, as so many assume, and should not give smart or perplexing answers to questions. The marker is there to help, not to hinder.

Any suggestion of a gesture should be avoided, such as walking up to the head as much as to say, when a bowl stops: 'There's an alteration now, don't you want to know about it?'

'Yes!' and 'No!' are standardised terms in marking: don't add anything to them without being asked.

Important to remember that only the player in possession of the mat can ask a question after the previous bowl has ceased to run.

Good markers make for a feeling of security for the players. But, after all, their duties are so simple, for they actually possess no rights, except palpably short jack throws, and crooked mat suggestions.

When a jack is thrown, and appears to be short, it should not be straightened until the prospect of a challenge is past.

When one player's bowl has stopped running, the next to play can ask a question from any part of the rink. No need to be on the mat.

As the scores are recorded on the card at the conclusion of each end, the marker should announce: 'Brown 10, Jones 14,' as the case may be, before leaving the head.

There are a few simple rules that, if observed, make marking satisfactory and easy for all concerned.

After straightening the kitty, retire out of the line of sight, and keep perfectly still until asked a question.

If asked who is shot, the reply should be 'You are,' or

'Against you,' without stating whether there are more shots than one, if such be the case.

Particularly, markers must be neutral. When one player walks up to view the head, don't hold any conversation with him in the absence of the other; walk away.

Markers who lean a little have been known to urge an opponent to 'get into the head' or 'put a fast one up.'

This or any other advice should be withheld in all circumstances. If a marker inclines towards one of the players, he should not display it.

Kicking bowls out before the players arrive at the head is strictly forbidden. Kicking them out at any time is the right of the contestants, to whom the game belongs.

An efficient marker deputes someone at the scoring board end to check the scores up, signalling right or left, according to who gets the shot or shots, at the same time registering the figures on the card.

Never turn a bowl over, or touch it, except to rub chalk off or chalk a toucher.

TEAM WORK AND OTHERWISE

SECOND and third men are often called upon to play a bowl here, or there, to secure position, and this necessary procedure does not fill them with enthusiasm or delight, to say the least. Many go so far as to say that the skip is keeping for himself a shot that he ought to ask them to carry out.

This is not teamwork! The tactics and strategy to be employed are in the hands of the captain, and at the end of a game, or the season, will reflect itself in the results.

A famous third man once called at the top of his voice to an equally famous skip: 'If you think I am going to place my bowls for you to run the kitty to, you have another think coming.' He subsequently got what was coming to him.

Many third men are of opinion that they should be given a vital shot, but forget that to do so would be premature, and allow the opposition to recover the position. Do as your skip orders; he does not keep the shot for himself, but for the side. Those thinking otherwise are better on the bank.

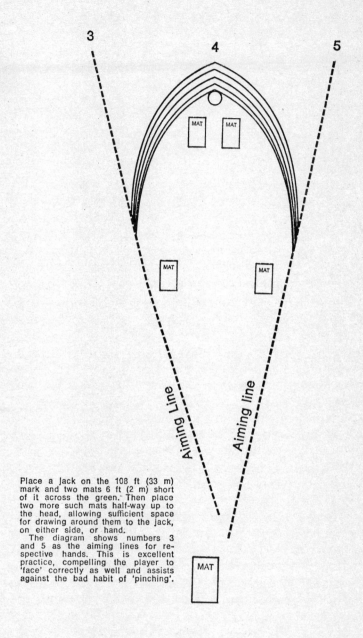

Place a Jack on the 108 ft (33 m) mark and two mats 6 ft (2 m) short of it across the green. Then place two more such mats half-way up to the head, allowing sufficient space for drawing around them to the jack, on either side, or hand.

The diagram shows numbers 3 and 5 as the aiming lines for respective hands. This is excellent practice, compelling the player to 'face' correctly as well and assists against the bad habit of 'pinching'.

LEADERS WHO NEVER MAKE CHAMPIONS

SHOULD an individual who has been taught to play an all-round game, at the inception of his career be called upon by selectors to keep laying the mat year after year because he has been an outstanding success in that role?

I say very definitely, 'No!' Invariably, after completing the education of a pupil, more particularly those with their best years ahead of them, my advice has been: Don't allow yourself to gain the reputation of not being capable of anything else but laying the mat.

A period in this department of the game is quite all right, but my opinion is that the older, used-up players should be listed almost exclusively as leaders. Some very sound reasons can be put forward in favour of this outlook. Let us take a case coming under notice that can be applied to almost all others.

A student, who came in at the age of 32, and who had shown great promise at the end of his educational term, complained that he was still kept laying the mat up to and after his third season.

'I have a good firm shot, and a good drive, and am versatile, generally,' he said. 'I merely stand round, after playing my two bowls, to see those following me perform much less efficiently than I could, and I am about fed up with this purely spectator role allotted me in every match.'

We all can place our hands on scores of leaders who have been kept mat-laying for 10 to 20 years on end. You don't find them in the list of competition winners, and when turning up press results of matches, scarcely ever look for or notice their names.

Rather, don't we invariably turn to see how many the skip is up, or down, who he is, and forget all about the poor leader, who probably lays the foundation of all his wins?

If you want to get anywhere on the game of bowls, don't 'star' as a leader only.

What use is their all-round play if they are never given an opportunity to demonstrate and maintain it in matches? With lack of opportunity, they soon lose their versatility, to become permanent mat slammers.

In due course they can say good-bye to the movements taught them, which include firm, firmer, fast, and faster shots, and all the fine points that go to make a first-class player. Why? Because they get no match practice, and fall into the leaders' monotonous groove.

One must lay this state of things at the door of selectors, many of whom contend that a young player should be kept at laying the mat for a few seasons before he is given a higher position. There are limits.

In his early career, the compiler of this treatise firmly (and successfully) contested this attitude to young enthusiasts. Had he not, it is fair to assume that his many activities, for good or ill, would have been non-existent.

Someone has to lay the mat admittedly, but why the young generation, except for a limited term? When the men whose sinews are not so elastic, who are feeling the stress of the years, but who can 'draw the shot with the next,' are available, they should be used exclusively as leaders, and are usually very reliable.

TRAPS THE UNWARY FALL INTO

Possibly the most effective means of rousing the average bowler from his bed of slumberous apathy and disregard for self-interest, or improvement, is to pelt him cordially with the jagged rocks of ridicule.

When you hurt a man's feelings in a good cause you do something for the cause.

The appalling and ever-increasing army of gropers, who drift into the game, and drift out as they came in, is a standing monument to the dual incapacity of the administering machine and the individual to strike out for himself. I say this with the road hog's 'excuse my dust' apologia, and pass on to further bends in the road.

The foregoing is written for a set purpose. There are hitherto undisclosed reasons why so many young bowlers develop 'driftitis' and finish at the tail end of the field.

After getting on right lines, they are approached by a type of reconstructor invariably well advanced in years, plus no recommendation except long experience in the game and a wholesome contempt for anything foreign to his own particular make-up.

A bit of this, that, and the other eventually causes them to strike out for themselves, with disastrous results. The man who does them the most harm is the admittedly good, prize-winning player, who gets there, not because of, but in spite of, his bad grip, incorrect stance, and false movements.

These men do the newcomer immeasurable disservice, and the poor souls who fall for the well-meant advice, imagine that any methods that bring success must be the correct ones.

The author knows many champions whom he would take his hat off to, but would be loth to recommend to a recruit. It is a mistake to assume that any man 'long in the game,' or having won an occasional event, should be accepted as an authority. That is the trend, and a dangerous one. All a question of the student's judgment.

Top and bottom spin, as practised arts in bowls, are just flights of the fancy. Don't chase these elusive mirages; they put nothing on the score card.

A high state of efficiency must be attained before departing from the rule of simplicity, and students are well advised not to add to their troubles.

The early run of a bowl after delivery is the weight you put into the action. The finishing run is the bowl's own weight. Study that out.

PUTTING POINTS ON THE BOARD

OUT of every bowl played from each end decided.

Out of any lapse, or lapses, on the part of opponent, or opponents.

Where a last-bowl-chance for a coup presents itself.

Out of the temporary disagreements, and consequent looseness of play, on the other side.

Out of the old adage that the discomforture of our friends is often not altogether displeasing to ourselves.

From Dame Fortune's fickleness, when the run of the game is going against the opposition.

When you know that the conditions do not suit the person, or side, you are engaged in playing.

Out of those that suit you best, by the same rule.

From observing that one or more of a four, or a singles player, is failing to 'get up' with his or their bowls.

From not being backward in taking advantage of the experience of others.

Out of a sweet-running green before the late afternoon slows it down.

When one hand is playing and the other is not, and before the other fellow switches over to it.

Out of your ability to 'smash up' an end, providing you have such ability.

From the lessons of defeat. To find out where you failed, and remedy the defects by practise alone.

Out of discovering where you should have drawn instead of having driven, or vice versa.

From the difference between concentrating upon the job in front of you, and chatting to those on the bank nearby.

When you are in the lead, and the other fellow chasing you, not you chasing him.

GOOD CURES FOR BAD FAULTS

BOWLS, of all the pastimes, must always be recommended. With good limbs, unimpaired brain, and sinews permanently stretched by the exercise daily, age, within reason, is no bar to championship class efficiency.

A good cure for the bad fault of round-arming your bowl, or looping it, is to be found in a smooth wall. Stand alongside and swing yourself out of the habit.

Confidence in yourself without the essential backing of ability is like owning the world's best car without spirit with which to propel it. You are no more able to go than the car, despite every up-to-date accessory the game has to offer.

Asking your man for a shot as you do it, or can do it, is not good policy. If you know him, even slightly, play him, not yourself, unless there is no option.

A very large percentage of bowlers are preference men. Even when it looks to be not the game, it pays to exploit their preference hand.

You alone know and have to decide how much time and concentration you need on the mat. Those who would have you 'go off' prematurely because their minds run in that groove, usually look after they have leapt, and it is too late.

Displaying impatience because someone is allegedly too slow, presents the latter with a powerful weapon, keeping the other up on his toes. Don't fall to the shrewd ones who spin for you in this connection by taking the bait.

You can have proved ideas and a set policy at bowls, which, indeed, is a necessity. That is no reason, however, why you should not depart from any and adopt those that look superior to your own.

There are talkers, whistlers, hummers and species of fidgeters, in the game. On the other hand, there are silent, immovable, 'saw-wood' individuals. These are paramount and provide most winners. The joker specimens are still joking when the tape is breasted.

'The more preparation you put on the bowl the less points you put on the board,' is not a truism, but it has a moral. The guess is on you.

There is variety in humans, as in flowers and plants. As with the latter, some are bright and fascinating, spreading their sweetness around, while others just as important, necessary, and useful, portray the Scotch thistle. It takes variety to make a satisfactory whole. If a rose, don't be disdainful of the marigold.

We are counselled not to use a light bowl 'because it can so easily be pushed out by the heavy ones.' Possibly the QCs of the sport overlook the fact that the light ones are just as easily pushed in, or up, as out. Likewise, the heavy bowl, just too short to count, will refuse to budge or be turned over once or twice by its more feeble brethren. And yet, for other reasons, the heavy bowls, like old things, are best.

There are master-minds (not too many of them) among greenkeepers. They should be the nurserymen for recruits. Greenkeeping is a profession embracing more than merely reflecting the green fields of Erin.

The man who can genuinely applaud a good effort by another he doesn't waste any affection upon politically, socially, or otherwise, reveals a trait in character much to be desired—and admired.

Pet aversions are what we make them. Prejudice against this or that make of bowl, some particular green or greens, personalities or officials in the game, etc, is a state of our mentality all the better for being put into reverse when it wants to go the most.

Talks, or lectures, on how to play the game of bowls are not the monopoly of anyone, but the man who would improve himself should exercise great caution in this connection. Theorists who have no solid backing from achievement are risky markets to speculate in, and should be given a wide berth. They might easily transfer their bad habits to others, in the belief that they are correct, but they cannot transfer their personalities. They are unconscious spoilers of careers.

Nobody obtains more satisfaction from a good deed than the benefactor. Even in bowls circles there are men who need a tonic for their drawbacks. It costs nothing to release a kind word that might end in an avalanche of reciprocity.

It is a mistake to assume that all those who do the measuring are in the same category as was Caesar's wife. The best method of preventing the stretch peculiar to the strings, and the stretching propensities of their users (not all, of course), is to abolish them by regulation.

Often the expression is heard: 'He was above himself,' or: 'Was much above himself on the day.' A player cannot be above himself. He can be at his best, which, after all, is a reproduction of what he is known to be capable of. Almost invariably these sentiments come from a defeated individual or side, and have to be accepted as a watering down of the other fellow's skill, in order to cover up someone's inability to defeat him.

No matter how expert a player may be, the day comes when he meets with defeat. Conditions and other things have their contributing factors, and so all there is left is to take it, with this reflection: It will serve to bring joy to someone.

To keep your balance (mentally) preserve your sight and nurse your nerves. Don't watch the opponent's bowls in their flight, in singles games! Doing so gets you up on your toes early, and in a long game is conducive to a weak and weary finish. I practise timing an opponent's effort as follows: Pick up the bowl, running the cloth over it while he is on the mat, and only look up when his bowl is finishing its course. You soon judge every effort to a nicety. Watch the opponent's feet; they are the index to what his brain thinks of the prospects.

If they become 'shifty,' or begin moving forward, he's in grave doubt. Actually, he's a moving picture for your benefit, saving you many a good fright.

BREVITIES

EVERY time you are beaten, look for the cause—it mostly presents itself. In most, if not all, of your narrow defeats, you can perhaps, recollect driving when you should have saved, or vice versa. It is all a question of bad or good judgment.

Dopes, tonics, needles, double-headers, to put pep or kick into you, before, or while a game is in progress are flights of fancy. 'Mind over matter' is a useful slogan in all tight corners.

A good brand of bowl grip is essential. Use that which will best give you the power to spin the bowl. All oily things are handicaps.

Never expect defeat. Tell yourself that the other fellow may be good, but he can't get inside the jack.

Silence begets good length; talk a lot, and you'll soon lose it. Make a point of showing your man that you don't want to talk; it can always be done diplomatically.

It is preferable to be convinced that you are wrong or weak in anything, to being compelled to by heavy defeat. The man who acknowledges his weaknesses or faults mends them soonest.

'Don't model your game after any particular player, but carve out your own destiny,' is an 'outer' on the target of approach in the bowls sport. Give such sentiment a wide berth.

A good loser is one who adroitly conceals the fact that he is seething within.

Defeat, when it comes, if not too often, is the same as a tonic to a healthy man; it assists in warding off the evils of assuming that 'these things can't happen to me.'

Fancy shots in competitive games are best left to the dreamers who stand them up, clips the bias in the draw, etc.

Don't attempt to fit fancies into the frames of realities; stick to simplicity and the beaten tracks of experience. That doesn't necessarily mean that 'what was good enough for grandfather is good enough for me.' You can be enterprising without being reckless.

We are told that we might as well physic the dead as argue with some people. By the same rule, we might as well whisper confidences into the ear of a corpse as try to convince the man who 'knows all there is to know' about any sport.

Constitute yourself a receptacle for information, good, bad or indifferent. Then separate the wheat from the tares, according to your judgment.

An open mind is a balanced mind. Don't close your eyes to your weaknesses, but go after them when someone points them out to you.

Look a bowler, if you are not even a class one. To be correctly attired not only stamps you as one who cares, but reflects credit upon your home folk.

You can't fool about and play well, at least for any length of time. Foolery spoils concentration. On the other hand, acquire a pleasantness within yourself that reflects itself in your exterior.

The leader who thinks he can choose his own length and play any hand he desires gets a lot of his own way, and it often pays to let sleeping dogs lie. The skip can sprag his wheel in both respects if he chooses, but mostly doesn't.

Many men have inherited the gift of 'taking it.' Others are handicapped, and can't 'take it' so easily. Don't be too ready to condemn the latter, they often possess virtues that you lack.

Ordering an opponent to return to the mat end, and stand six feet behind, after both had walked the full length of the green to view the head, prior to the delivery of the last bowl, is a form of insane overlordship aggravated by bad bowls law.

A demonstration of hand-clapping when an opponent in a fours or pairs makes an unlucky shot is bad taste and savours of a narrow outlook. Few men need this relevant reminder, however.

Recrimination is an irritant, and the aftermath of failure. Label it: 'Not to be taken.'

There is no art so easy of accomplishment as getting oneself disliked, particularly if one has a tendency to drive a wedge into the other fellow's defences.

That portion of the fingers and thumb, from the tips to the first joint, are the feelers from whence comes touch. Keep them soft, for the nerve sense is just under the skin. Those

144

people who propound other than the thumb and fingers on running surface should digest these facts. I confess to dogmatism in this respect.

The nonsense talked and written about rolling the bowl gently off the fingers, is thus further emphasised. The 'roll off' claim comes from the thumb-on-the-disc section of thought, which discredits itself upon examination.

Gentlemen's agreements in bowls consist of taking all that legitimately comes their separate ways, rejoicing internally at one another's lapses and embarrassments, and a total understanding that 'a clean slate' is not outside the range of possibility.

Slow-motion discloses that the bowl is spun, not rolled, and the spinning, life-giving agencies, are provided in the shape of the first joint of fingers and thumb, as aforesaid.

If you need any evidence to support these contentions, check up on the first palmer or sitter advocate, and note how he clasps a jack when throwing it (the full, or any length).

Possibly you love your garden because of the variety and colour it affords. It wouldn't be a garden if there was only one kind of plant or flower to be seen. So let us transfer our thoughts to the human plants that go to make up bowling club life. In that garden of souls variety is essential. If all thought, acted, played, and looked alike, it would be a drab, colourless assembly.

Opponents in the game are the partners in the business of building points in competitions. Each has his own commitments and draws as the need presents itself.

Men who 'never make mistakes' never make anything more than the noise necessary to proclaim themselves.

If bowls was not the 'lucky' game that it is, the bad and indifferent players would never win, and soon drop out. Its uncertainty is its charm.

The man who is 'no good to the club,' because he doesn't drink, is often a very much libelled individual, contributing in other ways preponderately in comparison with his detractors to the club's welfare.

'Going quietly,' when your opponent in a four bowl game beats you, is not only a courtesy, but a virtue. To proclaim

145

him—providing you mean it—stands you high up with the listeners.

Advice has recently been given to all and sundry by an ex-champion now retired to avoid taking objects on the bank as an aiming line, or point.

Here is positive proof that he is wrong: Assume that you are playing on rink 3, and that rink 4 peg is your green width, or line of aim, on the forehand on the day.

If I handed you a round bowl, instead of a biased one, and said to you: 'I have excavated a hole as big, and of the same size, as a motor-tyre, at No 4 peg; I will give you 50c every time you run this round bowl into that hole,' you would regard me as a philanthropist. It would be so easy.

Now, draw on your imagination, and assume that your biased bowl is a round one. But the bowl, if it could speak, might say when it reached three-quarters of the way:

'Excuse me, I turn off here to the left to pay my respects to Miss Kitty.'

Apply this to all your draw shots (and other shots, excepting for pace) and face shoulders, hips, knees, to make everything streamlined. This also includes the face of the bowl, its rings, the four fingers and thumb.

If I have been doing this for over forty years with the success you know, should that not prove its value, not to say necessity?

Is the last bowl in any game an advantage? Those who argue otherwise are not often found in the winning lists.

'Win the toss and throw the kitty' is some players' slogan. Give it to the opponent and conceal your length tactics, plus the last bowl, is ours.

A player who calls for a stimulant at intervals demonstrates two things: The first is inability to stand up to the game; the second a confession that he can't beat his man when normal.

Good players seldom play bad bowls on a good green, but bad players seldom play good bowls on a good green.

Most of our fears regarding opponents and their prowess, real or imaginary, vanish if we tell ourselves that we can't be reprimanded for losing. Don't dwell upon, or anticipate, defeat.

When the green is extra keen (16-18 sec) and the jack cut

over to, say, the right-hand boundary line, a trap is set that most players fall into. Judging the amount of the next rink that has to be taken is a difficult problem, and often results in the bowl becoming dead or useless if too wide. Play on the back hand well to the left of rink number peg.

Players with a 'preference' at bowls are those who prefer to play on a particular hand, because conscious of a weakness on the other. Check up regularly on your weaknesses and eradicate them.

Don't waste time and breath on anyone who argues that bad conditions are the same for one as the other, and that a good player should be able to master any kind of condition.

Brawn plays a very small part in the ancient game. The weakest, skinniest, most insignificant-looking individual has an equal chance with the giants of the flesh and muscle.

Players with an inferiority complex are bad match subjects. They look for ways out, get put off at the slightest pretext, see the mere waving of a cloth, or a turn-about by a skip, as something to fasten on to as an excuse for poor play. Confine them to social games.

Bowls is no more 'only an old man's game' than knitting is only an occupation for 'old maids.' The wars settled both questions definitely.

Draw-shots are the gilt-edged securities of the game and pay the best dividends. Driving by the man who is not expert is the medium of many calls in a year's operations.

You will be told that blocks are so many wasted bowls. The people who tell you so, after they crash into one or two, spend a lot of time working them out.

Claims for unearned points are almost invariably 'something for nothing' propositions, based on ignorance of the laws.

History proves conclusively that some of the best brains have made the biggest mistakes. Not one per cent of these claims is ever established.

Bad feeling is as undesirable as bad money, snobbery, or wealthy dictators.

Overrunning the head, after driving, is quite common, especially with elderly men, and is brought about by acceleration of the heart's action. Relax!

If there is any royal road to a successful career in bowls,

it can be summed up in two words: Systemisation, Standardisation.

Every proposition on a head is controlled by the same set of regulations governing the game. Obviously, then, it is absurd to suggest that a player should not employ fast shots for certain occasions or games.

There is considerable misconception regarding 'the pendulum swing.' On fast-running greens (16-18 sec) the action —full arm and shoulder—is a snare. On all smooth surfaces fingers and thumb, plus wrist action, give the best result. There is little or no touch in the full-arm method, as the nerves do not function so delicately. Of course, on slow greens (9-12 sec), particularly full-length heads, the pendulum comes into its own.

'Giving and taking' is a form of equity practised in the fields of British sport over all time, and will be till Eternity.

An apple a day may keep the doctor away, but a roll a day puts the medico out of court completely. Exercise is the foundation of health and a long life.

Avoid giving yourself away by a remark such as: 'I can't get that hand,' or 'These short lengths beat me,' etc. Your opponent puts shots on the board out of such admissions.

Split-second timing is one of the secrets of accurate driving. Brute strength plays a very small part.

A bowl will more readily do what is required of it if the fundamental principles of grip, stance, and delivery, as taught in this treatise, are not departed from.

Pity the third man who plays two bad shots himself, and upon crossing over hands out suggestions to the skip as to what he should do. His education has not been completed.

Knowledge, skill, and determination are the railroads to success at bowls. Getting on the jack is an art. Getting the other fellow off it is equally so.

It would be idle to pretend that the theories and lessons laid down in this book are cure-alls. There is no remedy for conditions that cannot be 'played' or handled.

'Gutters' will prevent any biased bowl from coming in on a head, just as other badly-levelled portions of a green will often cause the bowl to 'stand out' and not perform naturally as a biased sphere.

'A good shot, sir!' or 'Well played, my boy!' only costs a parting of the lips, and is sweet music to the listener.

Many bowlers are said to be very unpopular—an unmistakable tribute to their skill in the field.

The best stimulant in a hard game is courage, determination, and the will to win. Pick-me-ups are decoy ducks to defeat. 'Box on' under all circumstances.

No player, however bad, will acknowledge that he is as bad as the rest think he is. Such a trait is an advantage, rather than a drawback.

We are often too prone to rejoice at the downfall of a more than ordinarily good player. It is something in human nature not easy to define, but a thing of which we should not be too proud.

If you crash into a good 'block,' don't emulate the man who, having done so, said: 'You will get a lot of kudos for that, but it wasn't in the way.' Rather say: 'Well-placed, sir!'

Many are afraid to 'open their shoulders' because of the conviction that they will surely dislodge their own, one or more bowls, and leave the proverbial 'pot.' Eventually, this complex becomes so deeply rooted that caution turns to fear. While you may entertain it, don't allow the bogy-man to take up lodgings with you.

Choice of club colours should be left to good judges. Some mixtures suggest that their choosers were on the brink of delirium tremens at the supreme moment of deciding.

Taking green is a split-second determination of the vision prior to judgment of length. Don't look at the jack during this process.

When radical improvements were made in greens, bowls, rules, and perspectives, bowling ceased to be accepted as only 'an old man's game' for all time.

Nomination of low-grade players to act as selectors in a high-grade club represents a comedy as illogical as it is absurd. It is a species of egotistical dementia clandestinely whispered among the 'doctors who don't tell.' When an occasional selector of this order assumes control and proceeds to 'put the rule over' his victims, fermentation sets in, sooner or later. Personality selectors, like personality skips, should be confined to purely social activities.

High-class players in plenty, and years in the game, get there, and will continue so to do, not on account of correct methods, but by reason of their aptitude in overcoming drawbacks better left as such. They are a law unto themselves, but in odd cases a little reconstruction further improves them.

Peddling our virtues is merely encroaching upon the preserves of that ancient egotist who stood in the marketplace and thanked God that he was not as other men were.

No famous club ever became so by virtue of its social activities. First get on the map competitively, and the second leg will assuredly materialise. Promising players, and those who have been through the mill, are attracted to a competitively successful club, each being a unit that will build up the social structure.

Right-handed players will find that they will get better results from taking the backhand to the kitty when it is drifted close to up-and-down boundary line, at the right. The reason is that whereas the player must send his bowl into the next rink, if using the forehand (virgin country, really); with the backhand, his bowl is always in the rink.

In all walks of life—bowls included—there are people with an ever-ready negative for other opinions. They don't make good administrators, selectors, or even players.

Fledglings who are flat-out to fly in the cloudy skies of competition should not have their wings clipped by restrictions. Give them all the rope, scope and opportunity to practise on their own. In this connection, as is generally known, the writer devoted a whole year to study and practice, without restraint or interference, before entering the fields of competition.

There are two species of barracker: one who tells you something he can't withhold, and the one who withholds something he hasn't the courage to tell. The convincing grounds of the latter are street corners, where the victim is not in sight or hearing.

Confidence is something that hovers round everyone of us, but is a very timid creature, and easily frightened away. Retaining confidence is an art. Dress well, and natty, for your games; be afraid of no opponent; regard no shot as beyond you; box on till the numbers are up, and confidence will always be at your elbow.

MORE BREVITIES

CORRECT attire lends dignity and exclusiveness to a pastime in keeping with its traditions, and well worthy of our special attention.

Don't jump your hurdles before you come to them. Green's bad, of course, but it's just as bad for the others.

Confidence in yourself in anything spells contempt for the bogy-man who is tipped to beat you. In bowls it's essential.

Stiff people lose none of their awkwardness under high collars—don't wear anything but soft ones on the green.

'Don't hold your bowl like that,' said someone to one of our pupils. The retort courteous: 'It satisfies me, why should you complain?'

A bowl at the back is worth six at the front. You may be strong, but you won't offend.

A bowler in braces looks like a 'loud' sport who wants to be exclusive. Indeed, he is exclusive.

You may be down, but not half out—a player often 'comes from the clouds' to win.

Flukes, wicks, rubs, and all their tributaries are the sparks that spring from the plugs of uncertainty. They dazzle us and frazzle the opposition.

'Don't take down the shutters till you can display something attractive in the window'—a handy maxim for those who 'know' all there is to know.

Old players are never too old to learn. The author has picked up many points from those least expected to demonstrate them.

If your skip is a man who 'calls a spade a spade,' you will know he means it when he becomes demonstrative over your good efforts.

Why are the few infinitely superior to the many? A tour of the greens, and a passing glance at the multitude, will supply the answer.

Take advantages when they are fair, avoid doing so when they are doubtful, and scorn them when they are palpably unjustified.

Never, as in the past, and never in the future, will the

time-worn adage, 'It's the same for one as for the other,' hold good in any sport that calls for brain as against brawn.

Judging the shot at sight is a gift, and lamentably absent in many followers of the game. They don't make good markers in singles. Pick your man.

The competitive spirit is born in the wards of efficiency. The efficient go after it; the inefficient, or purely social, tell us they don't play in these club events. The reason is apparent.

If personal qualities in a skip come before ability to play any shot (as some propound) be accepted, personal quality classes would soon take the place of schools for learning. Don't fall for such rubbish.

An acknowledgment that you can be put off any particular effort is an admission you should not advertise. Don't allow this complex to develop.

Writers have for centuries been telling third men not to interfere with the captain's prerogative. Wise thirds, like hen-pecked husbands, don't say over-much.

To be in the limelight is very illuminating. Better to occupy a subordinate position in a champion four with a good chance than be skip of a four with no chance.

Diplomacy is a mixture of sincerity, deceit, tact, and ex-pediency. It allows sleeping dogs to lie, bowlers to display their superiority, and dictators to expound their knowledge. It bides its time, and steps in at the right moment. Be a diplomat if your conscience allows.

Bias begins to act just prior to the first turn in the finishing run. Keep this in mind on fast greens.

In order to prevent bowling narrow on either hand, get the habit of facing shoulder square to the boundary pegs at first.

There is a story behind the personal appearance of most bowlers, seldom or never told—the 'love' work of someone, unseen—and appreciated—by outsiders.

Playing to the rules, but giving away a little where the rules do not apply, makes for harmony and good-fellowship.

Before beginning a singles game, have an understanding with the marker or scorer. Inform him that the players will, or will not do the measuring, and get his definition of when a bowl is jack high.

It often happens that a marker or scorer is sympathetically

disposed towards your opponent. Cases are on record of them actually urging the player to do certain things when he walks to the head to inspect. Make it a habit to walk to the head with him.

'I've been leading all my life,' is not an uncommon wail. There must be some grounds? Plenty are not ambitious, and are content to stay mat-layers; others, who would never fill any other job efficiently, clamour for higher positions. If you don't want to be a lead 'for the term of,' improve your game in the finer points.

There are several classes of driver, and there are reasons why each is different from the other. The 'daisy-cutter' greens his bowl low, and is a good timer, because he gets right down to it. He is uncommon. Dumpers are plentiful. They don't bend either knee or spine overmuch, and 'hit' the earth as a consequence. Get worse with age as well.

'I prefer a bending, firm shot to any kind of a drive, and recommend this policy to others,' wrote one of our regular contributors to the game. He is not the only one. Poor chaps, they overlooked the cold fact that there are positions daily, on all greens where a firm shot must become 'wrecked' before reaching the vital point of a head. When these fits of philanthropy strike them they should be sure that their readers are all badly informed, for how few but don't know that bending shots cannot possibly reach certain lies on a green—impossible to get at only per medium of a straight one?

Ditches without sand are emblems of neglect, demonstratons of carelessness and monuments of disinterestedness.

Some bowlers bring off a 'king' fluke and declare that they played for it, rather than acknowledge the truth. Don't be too hard on them; their own consciences do all that is necessary later.

Be indulgent to the man who has to be 'wound up' to do himself justice. He may be a 'bit of a crank' when in that state of mind, but is mostly a good fellow, with high ideals and spotless character in private life. Who can afford to judge him harshly, anyhow?

The game is the thing; don't drag it down to a level its detractors would present it to you. Any of the sporting games can be (and, unfortunately, have been) so burlesqued as to

153

make good copy for cheap jibers who find their way on to newspaper staffs at times. If you possess a good name, see that its dignity and high standard is maintained.

Men who appeal mostly to the writer are those who, being more than average good players, seek improvement from anyone competent to assist them, and who are not too proud to acknowledge the service.

Markers, with extra long legs, very often take two strides of 3 ft 6 in (106 cm), and then place the white at the tip of their shoe—about 7 ft 6 in (2 m) instead of 6 ft (2 m) when the jack is thrown close to the ditch in singles play.

Don't join that little band of irreconcilables who periodically tell you things contrary to accepted teaching. They mostly constitute the never-win, but not the *savoir faire* (skilful) section of the bowls game.

If you are playing a competition match and conform to the usual courtesies and code regulations, winning is all there is to it.

Some players are unable to conform to the grip as laid down in these pages. They are not expected to, for the reason that freak thumbs prevent them doing anything else than dropping that member to the side of the bowl. These are few, however.

That apparition of the brain we call 'fancy' comes largely into the picture, silently, but patiently persuading the all-too-absorbent subject that he can do better for Placidity Peter than Dynamic Dave. Whatever the cause, many men do give better service to some than to others, and this should be a theme for selectors. The opinion that one skip has better control over inferiority complex cases than another cannot be ruled out.

In any game an opponent gets only as many points as you allow him to get.

A player may beat you on the day, or periodically, and still not be your master. In arriving at values, consistency counts.

There is usually a good hand to a bad rink. It pays to play it, even though enemy short bowls block the way. Many matches are won and lost by forcing opponents on to the bad hand. To be a consistent winner you must play the conditions, whatever they may be, a bit better than the other fellow.

Always play the shot as you see it—as you would if practising in a roll up. Many allow an important occasion or match to get their morale, and depart from what should be a golden rule.

When you encounter that creepy feeling that denotes funk, tell yourself that it's only a game of bowls, and you'll feel better and regain confidence. More games are lost by funk than through any other avenue.

Loosely tied or sloppy shoes are a menace to your game. Feel well ribbed up all over.

A clean take-off is essential to spin. Make certain that just exactly where you are going to grass the bowl is smooth and the grass undisturbed. A good plan and an allowable one is to press the part with the sole of your foot. Rough take-offs cause many short bowls, depriving them of necessary revolutions.

If you are drawn to meet a champion, or any whom you imagine might make you look cheap, don't turn up his record or allow the fact that you have to meet him disturb you. It is bad to dwell upon a big game ahead—take them in your stride.

There's a time and place for everything. Don't leave the green when you are 'wound up' to have a drink. If you or your opponent must have one, ask someone to bring it out.

Whatever your object is in taking green, be it on the bank or playing-surface, play at it, not to it.

Every player of note has, or should have, a set policy. At the expiration of three or four ends you should know what hand is best and what to avoid. Don't fight a bad hand, it's a losing game.

People who argue that driving does not pay, or that it should be barred, broadcast their own shortcomings. If an opponent can't drive you have no need to place back bowls.

A leading player-writer of South Africa wrote: 'Short blocks are a waste of good material.' An equally good player, after a 25-17 defeat in Australian Pairs Championship at Perth (final), said: 'Those short blocks were an object lesson to us, they looked as big as tanks to me [skip] and my partner.' What is the inference? The South African was evidently not a case for the short block—the WA men were. You have to find out your opposition, and act accordingly. The South

155

African dictum only applies when the subject is not a case for the block.

A fatalist (at bowls) is he who doesn't think he can do it. The optimist is he who knows he can't do it—but keeps the knowledge to himself, in case he flukes it.

A very good question to put to the average marker in a singles game is: 'What is the position?' The man of forced silence can then let himself go (as one recently did), and preach a regular sermon about it.

Players who see movements at the other end get upset by the shifting of a leg, a puff of smoke from a cigarette, or a dozen other flights of the imagination, should put on their considering caps.

He who thinks aloud is preferable to the silent worker species. The man who tells you is a lift on the road to repentance; take his 'lambastings' as you would mint sauce with roast lamb. If only a short in the game, don't begin telling till you are competent to do so.

STILL MORE BREVITIES

Specialising for any particular player, by a skip, is a form of strategy almost wholly neglected. A wide-awake captain notes that either his No 2 or 3 is consistently playing strong or short. He then asks his leader to throw the jack that length.

Time limits and 'ringing-off' players from the green is not the kind of thing for men known as 'elderly,' and it is foreign to the outlook of most. Anticipation of the bell acts upon the nerves, and limits play into the hands of pointers.

Some players are branded as 'too keen.' This keenness is commendable rather than condemnable.

The run of the game is often the deciding factor between success and failure. It is a form of predestined happening for which there is no cure, and which curriculums studiously avoid.

Several feet of bias can be taken off a bowl by holding it with a cant and delivering it so that when it reaches the green the point of contact is approximately the inner large ring of the bowl.

Some exhibit a curious, sulky display of antagonism when a head is smashed, but appear joyful if the effort fails.

If you drive and miss your object, then the antis take the
floor, and tell you that 'it's not the way to win';
But when you hit the target, it's not 'skittles' any more;
just the silent frame of mind you catch them in!

Don't play 'ditch theory' (jack on the 6 ft (2 m) mark and mat near centre of green), against a versatile opponent who is liable to pop the white into the ditch at any moment and leave you stranded.

Bowling institutions serve as opportunity clubs as well as their other social uses. Scattering seeds of kindness for their reaping by and by can be accomplished as the opportunities present themselves. Don't allow the clergy a monopoly of this commodity.

Perpetual shifting of the pegs, and producing grass by indiscriminate flooding, is not greenkeeping. 'My green is the same, and level all over,' is a slogan experienced players don't fall for.

Some clubs are like the Blue Alsatian Mountains, they not only remain stationary, competitively, but merely watch and wait while others progress. They stand out from their inability to stand in—pyramids of inactivity.

A nippy contortionist, smile-producing player takes drabness out of a sport that hitherto has been considered too drab for serious thought by the younger set. If anyone in particular is a 'showman,' he gives pep to the game and gets our pat on the back for it.

Insure against risk with a bowl at the back. Flukes are the sparks that fly from the anvils of uncertainty. Be insured, the premium is low.

A well-placed short block is the spider's web of bowls. It catches big and little alike.

If you are 'not much to look at,' like the chap who started life at the log cabin, and finished at the White House, you can still be 'a beggar to go.' Not always the stylist takes the prize.

The difference that a sodden surface makes (as against a keen one) to many high-class players is so marked that they appear to be out of form, or to have slipped. It is always dangerous to assess values from heavy green performances.

157

Practise this at home on the carpet: Take an ordinary chair, turn the back to where you are assumed to be delivering a bowl. Place left hand on top of chair, after stooping to your usual moulding. Hold the bowl out in front on the poise, and say: 'O-n-e,' well drawn out, as you swing it backwards. When you swing it forward, say, 't-w-o,' and you will get perfect timing. Swing must be unbroken.

If you desire to wreck your opponent's locomotive, place a 'sleeper' on his line; in other words, a block a little more than half-way between the mat and his objective.

Fast shots are the dive-bombers of bowls; they crash into packed heads, and spread consternation among the ranks of 'the enemy.' Indiscriminate driving, however, often ends in a crash of a different order. Don't stunt!

The alleged pot-hunter is a person who has built, or is building up, a record, and possesses a natural desire to add to it. Those who cast sneers at him are the types of failures whose outlook on the successful ones detracts from the value of their accepted good points in other directions.

Friendships made on the bowling greens are too precious to be lost. Keeping them is a pleasant kind of hobby, surely?

It cannot be too often stressed that successful players do not necessarily measure up as coaches.

It is the province of novices and would-be improvers to select their mentors, many of whom have been operating as such for years.

A horse-trainer is known by the winners he turns out, and this applies to the bowls coach.

Looking for results at the other end is futile if we don't do the correct thing by the bowl at the mat end.

Beware of the friend who tells you that you are only a one-hand player. 'You used the fore-hand all day, pretty well; do you lean to it?' was a query put to the author after a day on an Auckland (NZ) green. A good lesson lay in the reply: 'I used the fore-hand only because it was the hand on all rinks that was playing, and by the same rule would have used the back hand in like circumstances.'

'Chipping-in' leaders or seconds who constantly urge the Number Three to get the skip to do this, or play that, should be labelled dangerous, upsetting, or troublesome in the mental albums of all those responsible for including or excluding them for selection.

The open air, the society of our friends, the bloom of the flowers, and the stretches of forgetfulness from business, domestic or professional worries, are the unseen and unhandled ingredients that emerge from the greatest of all games, bowls.

The culminating point of argument is surely achievement? The latter, in its turn, is the unalterable and irrefutable verdict of the jury. No argument is complete without a showdown, whether it be in relation to runner, boxer, tennis, golfer, or bowls player.

Therefore, in order to arrive at values when records come up for discussion, achievement is the only sound basis. Periods, places, opportunities, and the want of them certainly have to be taken into consideration.

A bowl will act only in accordance with what you do to it. Dump it, and it becomes a dull, leaden thing. Spin it, and life springs from the action. Wobble it, and anything can happen.

Controlling bodies everywhere should taboo 'freak' competitions and frown upon such things as a penalty of one point for a dead end. They should demand that the code, and nothing but the code, be followed, submitting all programmes to scrutiny.

'Taking the bit' is a form of rebellion practised by players who appear to think that the captain at the other end is there merely for his vocal qualities.

Human nature is a mass of contradictions. The section of it that is prejudiced against the drive shot inwardly prays that you won't employ it when there is a bunch lying in their favour. History cremated them long since.

In order to obtain the maximum of sympathy (touch) between the nerve sense and the bowl, that film we know as skin should be kept as soft and thin as possible. Sedentary subjects have an advantage here.

There are two important fundamentals connected with winning: one is physical condition; the other, competitive spirit. The latter is usually much undeveloped in the social bowls devotee.

When a bowl is played a few inches directly beyond a jack,

make the wings the next objective, rather than an Aunt Sally for the opposition.

Many points and matches are lost by overbuilding a head. The order 'Come up to it,' is the outcome of such crowding.

The man, or men, you are playing should be subjects for quiet study as soon as a game begins if the latter be worth the while. One-hand players, objects for the block, short or long end 'cases,' those with a bending shot, but not a straight drive, should come within the category.

Whether players win titles per medium of the drive or lose them by the same route, is a question that cannot be answered by reference to any particular man or men. History shows, and will continue to show, that not more than 1 per cent 'all-draw' exponents win a classic singles. Those who know this and still fail to reconstruct (where possible) will always be the rearguard of the competitions.

Silent partners in a pairs match, and often a fours game (except when the skip asks for directions), put more points on the score card than all the 'orators' on the other rinks put together.

Laying the mat with the rough in front is an act of the unobservant. It spells anything but *bel esprit*, and says *au revoir* to spin, life, and length. Laid with a smooth, clean take-off, on the other hand, confidence and the art of correcting is maintained. Leaders are the worst offenders.

Assurance is a specialty in the average English-speaking subject. When he asserts that you 'fluked him,' or that he should have won, remember the characteristic in the great invasions.

'Pick up the bowl naturally, and allow it to sit comfortably in your hand' is not expert advice, and should be treated accordingly.

If your club is fortunate in its greenkeeper, no price within reason is too high to pay for his retention. By the same rule, curators who are merely producers of green grass are dear at any price.

The time occupied in the process of picking up your bowl, walking on to the mat, and delivering it, is all your own, and should not be cut short to suit the critic who would hasten the effort. The reasons are also your property; retain them if satisfied that they are sound.

Always be on the alert for the unexpected. It has a habit of hiding behind a corner, then surprising everybody by a sudden appearance. The one most concerned, usually, is the player who has the game 'won,' and who has ceased to regard the other fellow seriously. In the future, as in the past, 'a game is never lost until it is won,' will stand. Underrating an opponent has brought many a man to grass in all arenas of life. Don't regard any as a Juggins until you prove otherwise, and then keep the information for future assessments. 'I foolishly relaxed,' says many a loser. All right if it passes the censor, but is mostly a fairly safe exit from a bad showing. These 'smother-ups' rarely reach their intended destination. A more popular one might be: 'He was just too good, and that's all there is to it.'

The mat is a mound from which we fire all our shots, good, bad, and indifferent. The targets are the heads, from which 'bulls,' 'outers,' and 'misses' are registered.

Blocking is a much-neglected art. Never look at anything but the spot you desire your bowl to stop at in making any kind of block, then take the necessary green (3-4 ft or 1-1.5 m), and draw to that spot.

In bowls, as in other sport, we need the showers of knowledge. But we can't fill our reservoirs of information from them if we are outside the catchment area.

A good thing to remember is that if you move a bowl or the jack when measuring, it is always your opponent who then has to act, not you. So be careful.

Most of our problems in the game are added to by an acceptance at the outset than we can't do this or can't do that. Failure to curb such spirit of abandon encourages the growth of an inferiority complex that we all more or less possess.

'That club spirit' is a good one when there is no catch in it. Many propound the virtue for their own unseen ends.

Delicacy of touch is a product of the unity of nerve and brain. It is the highest trump card of the bowler's pack. The soft ball of the fingers and thumb are the feelers to length and strength, further emphasising the advantages of the grip propounded in these pages. Medical history reveals that the

161

second, or longest, finger has been the feeler employed for problems that have confronted the profession. To those to whom trifles loom large on the landscape of thoroughness, the author offers this recipe: Keep those touch agents soft and pliable. Wash the hands in warm to hot soapy water as a habit, thus establishing the thinnest of films between bowl and nerve sense.

Objections from the bank, to anything allowed by the rules, are sometimes based on a too correct observation of such rules. It is a good thing to be with the bank, as then it is mostly with you. All a matter for individual discretion.

YET MORE BREVITIES

DOES cigarette or pipe-smoking during a game spoil concentration? No! Neither does it put any points on the board.

Getting rattled is a state of the mentality not only peculiar to bowlers; it is to be found among all types of sportsmen, and has no relation to an inferiority complex. Surrendering to something we can't see, but feel the effect of, possibly covers the condition.

Don't practice on a heavy or uncut green. The woodheap or the front lawn affords ample exercise, and somebody is made glad.

Take your bearings before you step on to the mat, otherwise make up your mind about the shot and hand you will play, then go to it. This prevents after-regrets. In this connection, don't dwell upon what the bank may think if you delay a little. The bank is merely the wall the picture hangs on, you being the painter.

Nobody should deny the right of others to take the game other than from an angle of indifference or unconcern. When we hear a man say that he plays the game merely for the social enjoyment it affords him—as so many do—rest assured that his standard is such that enjoyment is all there is left for him.

Congratulating an opponent immediately following defeat and the natural disappointment it often entails, is a courtesy indispensable to the game.

Don't remain a tenant in a tumble-down house, and don't

admit 'can't' into the passages of your vocabulary. 'Never too late to mend,' the most elderly of the multiplicity of maxims, still stands, like the white cliffs of Dover, pre-eminent.

It is important to remember that all scoring measurements are made from the nearest point of a bowl to the nearest point of the jack. However, in a jack length challenge and a 6 ft (2 m) from the front ditch placement the measurements are taken along the surface of the green, as this is the only correct way to measure the position of a sphere on a plane surface.

It is established beyond doubt that a large percentage of players are weak on one hand or the other. These should be subjects for close observance.

If all men are equal on the green, as beneath it, as alleged, preferences should automatically accrue to those best qualified to receive them.

While 'there'll always be an England,' there will always be a game called bowls for old men. No other is in sight, or ever likely to be, that could provide the outlook, exercise, social intercourse, friendship and all else our ancient pastime has to offer.

Not a few players, when stepping forward, come down with a flat foot. That is a sure sign of premature movement of the left leg. (This applies to right-handers, of course.) The leg should be restrained until the bowl is brought back to the maximum, and then allowed to go with limbs moving at the same moment.

Many players, originally inoculated with the wrong serum by well-meaning but inefficient practitioners, have to be born again into the game and enter the nursery of reconstruction. Some respond to treatment and make bonnie bowls babies, but most fail to reach maturity. Prevention being better than cure, pick your practitioner; don't let him pick you.

Getting 'up on our toes' on the day of a singles match, and prior to the event, is a state of mind produced by dwelling upon it. Be casual; don't dwell!

Have you ever studied the relation of the soles of your bowling shoes to the mats in use at the time being? Red rubber, for instance, slips badly on coconut matting, and certain other material used for shoes soles doesn't go with duck.

Tightly-laced shoes, especially across the nearest point to

the instep, beget confidence, steady the whole frame, and prevent rocking of the body.

Old friends see the best that is in us by virtue of their knowledge of us generally. This fact, in turn, calls forth our best efforts.

Avoid, at all costs, what we term an inferiority complex. A close study of those who possess it reveals the fact that their morale is within your grasp. A player with this disability cracks up before any other.

Determination is mostly inherited, but can be acquired. Lack of it in bowls is a tragedy. Don't be too ready to admit you are beaten or show that you feel creepy; nothing will spur your opponent on more. Keep a stiff upper lip, though your bowling heart breaks.

Don't pretend to members of your rink if they are intelligent men. Better to remain silent with a bad shot than encourage them with something you cannot possibly mean. Then, when approbation comes eventually, they know you are sincere.

Over-running the head after driving is a common fault. It is largely physical. Drop the arms immediately after a heavy drive, and allow the arm muscles to get back to normal.

Bowls with an exaggerated uncontrollable draw, in the hands of a mediocre player, are like fools with too much money.

Methods for taking the bias off in fast driving, swerving, and 'standing them up' are not part of the author's curriculum —they have to be acquired by practice.

Play to the rules invariably, always being ready to give and take in small matters that have no bearing on the result. There are times when a concession means only a courtesy.

Opinions are the expression of thought, their value being assessed according to the source from which they spring.

Some simply cannot lose well, despite laudable intentions to that end. Don't be too ready to remind them of it.

Getting the other fellow's goat is an art mostly practised by 'gentlemen' with nothing else to distinguish their personalities.

No game is lost till the final numbers are up. It is a good thing to keep that proverb in mind. Too many players are inclined to think that they have no chance, and are morally beaten before they start.

Someone has said that 'there is no royal road to honour rolls.' There is! Not only for the reason that I found it in my first year, but because it is there for anyone to find.

Little pinpricks and staged episodes upset equilibriums. Don't be upset. The actors will soon tire of staging them if you show unconcern.

The poorest tribute you can pay to a man of outstanding ability, in any walk of life, is to declare that he has no enemies.

The best way to overcome a preference is to admit you have one, and to practise on the hand you don't prefer.

When the author was three or four seasons in the game, and had taken all the titles, he thought he 'knew,' and chafed at playing under successful men. Ripe experience taught him many things essential to the leading of men, and that his early premises were erroneous. Don't jump your obstacles till you come to them.

Prizes won from a bank seat never reach the sideboard. Such onlookers as can always do something those on the green fail to accomplish are often the biggest duds in the game.

Bowls bank-seat psychology is a state of mind possessed by those who are not playing at the moment or who don't play at all.

Suitable, close-fitting underwear keeps the soft muscles together, and nurses the nerves. Be well-ribbed-up underneath.

THE BOWL YOU PLAY WITH

HAVING dealt with the game from every possible angle, this volume would not be wholly complete without special reference to the material the bowling community had used and which it is using at the present moment, embracing the drawbacks of the former and the advantages of the latter.

In dealing with the question of what bowl I favour—and I have been asked that question hundreds of times, verbally and per mail—it is only fair to say that the product of R. W.

Hensell and Sons Pty Ltd has been my ideal, and is undoubtedly the most perfect bowl yet made. Indeed, the record I have established could not have been built without it. The scientific precision of the bowl is one of its outstanding features.

What I admired is the perfection with which the finished bowls run on the testing table, the machining process being so perfect that the bowls are automatically biased and balanced as they come from the machine.

After polishing and engraving each set is stamped to comply with the regulations in the countries where the bowls will be used.

I present this story merely as a grand finale to my instruction and advice. It is not the province of this treatise to stipulate what make of bowl anyone should use or not use; but for those who lack the facilities or experience to choose for themselves there is an infallible guide: Look up the records of the past years and note what the title-winners have been using. Success of anything or in anything is usually a reliable fingerpost.

APPRECIATION

No greater tribute could be paid to the compiler than to persuade him to produce further editions in order to satisfy the public demand. Their appearance signifies the termination of my mission, and, in the bowls sense, one feels that he can say with Gordon: 'I would live the old life over if I had to live again.'

Many there are, competent to criticise, who do not subscribe to all views and methods as expressed in these pages, and those of previous editions, but the best evidence of universal acceptance comes from a quarter most competent to pronounce judgment, viz, the big distributing houses of the world. They are unanimous that the book stands pre-eminent.

Comme il faut.

THE ETIQUETTE OF BOWLS
By
The Late J. P. MONRO, B.A.
(Noted bowls historian and former Hon. Secretary of the Royal Victorian Bowls Association)

THE most expressive definition of Etiquette is "conventional decorum". It is those little acts that help to make Our Game such a wonderful creator of sociability and friendship.

Etiquette is not an explanation of the duties of the various players in the team; but it is those little extras that give to the Royal, Ancient and Agreeable Pastime its great charm; that make the loser feel he has not lost in vain; that lead one to believe there is even a sweetness in defeat. These acts of courtesy are the Unwritten Laws of the Game.

There is an Etiquette to be observed towards our opponents; there is an Etiquette obligatory to and from Markers and Umpires; there is an Etiquette observable between players and spectators.

ONE'S OPPONENT

It is a nice gesture to commend a good bowl of your opponent, and of a player in your own team; you will find that he will do the same to you. It is etiquette to admit a fluke in a good spirit, with such a remark as "We all get them, and they're very welcome when they come!"

If you have arranged to play a match (say in the Club Championship) with your opponent, you must refrain from practice on the green that day. No competitor in a Singles should practise on the green on which he is drawn to play at any time after the draw for that day's play has been made, unless he has a bye, or is given a walkover, in which case he may play four ends on a rink in which he was drawn to play (in the walkover), or on a rink being available when he has a bye. It is not etiquette to follow your bowl with the object of obstructing your opponent's view of the run of the bowl. Distracting the attention of a player when he is about to bowl should not be done.

167

Do not keep your opponent waiting if a time has been fixed for commencing a match; if prevented by any unforeseen circumstance from being punctual, send a telephone message to him as to the time you will be at the green; if you do not turn up, he may rightly claim the match.

The loser should be allowed the privilege of being the first to congratulate the winner.

No player should delay play in a match by leaving the rink without the consent of his opponent or of the opposing Captain; and then only for a period not exceeding ten minutes.

ATTIRE

To maintain the general appeal which the game manifests throughout its adherents, a standard of dress is laid down by the rules and this uniformity adds dignity and charm to the playing of the game of bowls.

In bowls fixtures, whether competitive or social, gentlemen players must wear white or cream trousers; white or cream socks and white or tan smooth rubber (or other approved material) soled and heel-less shoes.

The wearing of white or cream shorts to an approved design is permitted under varying control of the State Authority and if shorts are worn, long white or cream socks must be worn.

Shirts, white or cream, may include the State badge insignia on the left breast pocket if approved by the State Authority.

Hats and caps of approved design, white or cream and the appropriate State blazer and tie may also be worn.

Cardigans, jackets and pullovers, white or cream, may be edged with the State's colours or colour to approved dimensions.

Ladies' attire is an all white frock of approved design and length with short or long sleeves; white smooth rubber (or other approved material) soled and heel-less shoes with stockings — the colour of which vary in each state but generally, of a "mini-beige" colour. White hats must be worn with or without a dark green underlining on the brim.

Cardigans or jackets as approved, may be worn with appropriate State blazer when necessary and additional accessories, only as approved.

THE LEADER

In tossing, it is the home player who spins the coin, and the visitor who calls.

It is a very nice custom and of the best etiquette for a player in a Singles, or a Leader in a Pairs, Triples or Fours, while his opponent is laying the mat, to pick up the jack and the opponent's bowl and to hand them to him when the mat has been laid, holding the jack in the left hand and the bowl in the right hand when delivering them to a right-handed bowler. This little act immediately places the two opponents on very friendly terms.

In a Pairs the Leader does the measuring. That's his job. It is not etiquette for the Captain (skip) to go to the head and interfere. Matches may be lost through defective judgment on the part of the measurer. On the other hand, the opposing Leader — knowing this weakness on the part of his opponent — should not take advantage of it, and claim a shot or shots that are not rightfully earned.

THE SECOND

Before a Fours match commences, it is the practice for the home Second to introduce the players to each other, and for the players when introduced to mention their respective Christian names with a remark such as "My name is Tom," or "My friends call me Jack."

The Captains are the first introduced, then the Leaders, the Seconds, and the Thirds, in that order. In some clubs it is customary to introduce each player to every opponent.

If you are a Second, it is required of you to compare with the opposing Second the scores at the conclusion of each end; to see that the score-cards are initialled at the completion of the match; and if you are the home player it is your job to attend to the score-board during the progress of the match, and at its termination.

THE THIRD

When playing Third, and it is a question of measure, let your opponent have the option of measuring; and if it is a long measure you should assist him by holding one end of the stick, steel tape, or whatever means is employed.

If your Leader or Second draws your attention to a shot that you have overlooked, thank him; it is the team that is playing and an overlooked shot may mean the loss of the match. If your opponent is overlooking a shot in his favour, suggest that it may also be in the count; that is a generous interpretation of Etiquette, and one much appreciated, for bowls is a game of good sportsmanship.

The Third has no right to tell the Captain what to do; he may advise him if the head has been altered after the Captain has left it, but he must not control his play. The Etiquette in this case is for the Third to remain silent until the Captain asks for advice. It is the Third's job to indicate to his captain the result of the end by raising or lowering his right hand, showing with his fingers extended the number of shots obtained for or against. The gesture of the Third in recovering his Captain's bowls from the ditch (or wherever they may be) and placing them close to the mat will be appreciated by the "Skip". If it is your Captain's turn to bowl, the placing of his bowl on the mat will be helpful to him.

THE CAPTAIN

When you are a Captain, remember that the men in your team are as anxious to win as you are, and that is bad form to remind any of them that he has put down a bad bowl — he knows that equally well as you do; and it hurts him more if you remind him of it by word, grimace or action. Remember, also, that all bowlers (including Captains) play bad bowls at times, and lose games, too. Cheap sarcasm or disparaging remarks as to the play of their men, or of their opponents, are not expressed by good bowlers.

A Captain may be gracious enough at the crossover to confer sometimes with his Third as to the shot he proposes to play. When on the mat the wise Captain will ask his Third for advice as to the position if the head has been altered since he left it. It is good policy, and also good Etiquette, for a Captain to commend the play of his men, and the good shots of his opponents, without being too lavish about it. And it is also correct for the Captain to indicate to his men at the mat end the position after the Leaders, Seconds and Thirds have played their bowls.

It is a nice practice for a Captain to pick up his opponent's bowl and hand it to him when he is about to get on the mat; and reciprocity of this gesture will likewise be appreciated.

THE TEAM

Now let us consider the Team. The Laws of the Game and Etiquette require that the players at the mat end — other than the player actually playing his bowl — shall, wherever possible, stand a distance (in Australia at least 2 metres — approximately 6 feet) from the back of the mat; and when at the head the players other than the Directors shall stand (in Australia at least 2 metres — approximately 6 feet) behind the head. When a player is about to deliver a bowl, Etiquette requires that those at the head shall not move about. Morever, the opponent or opponents must not be annoyed by those playing against them.

If a maimed or limbless bowler, or one otherwise handicapped, happens to be playing against you, Etiquette demands that you attend to him by picking up his bowl, or holding his sticks or crutch while he is delivering his bowl, and generally by making this game as pleasurable as you can. He did his part on the field of battle; you do yours on the field of play.

If you are playing on your home green against a visiting team, Etiquette requires that you should, at the afternoon tea adjournment, accompany your opponent and attend to his wants. You must pay for him and for yourself. Later on the visiting player must not omit to "return the shout". Hardly anyone is as despicable as the "shout-dodger".

When crossing over from the mat to the head, be careful to confine yourself to the rink, and not trespass into the adjoining territory and thus cause annoyance to other players. Endeavour, too, when you have played your bowl not to follow it more than the prescribed distance beyond the mat-line, and see to it that you do not cross into the adjoining rink.

If you borrow a measure, a pencil, or even a piece of chalk, be careful to return it to the owner. Do not argue with the Captain about the shot to be played; it is the correct thing to wait until you are asked before expressing an opinion. If you are the Captain, do not "butt-in" when the Thirds are measuring — it is their job to determine the shot, not the Captain's. If you are the Leader or the Second, and the Captain asks the Third what the position is, or how many shots there are for or against him, remain silent; it is the Third's job to answer

171

the question; moreover, the Leader or the Second must not wave his arms about to indicate the shot to play or the likely score.

It goes without saying that it is decidedly bad form for any bowler to use bad language during a match or elsewhere. Bowls is a game of good sportsmanship.

BOWLERS GENERALLY

Every intending member of a club has to go through the routine of being nominated, seconded and elected (or otherwise) after a prescribed period. Before he is nominated his proposer should explain to him what pecuniary obligations are entailed — the subscription to the club, the cost of a set of bowls and case, the locker fee (including insurance), etc.; what the correct attire is, and generally how the club is managed.

When he is elected it is the duty of the member who nominated him to take him in hand, show him round the club, introduce him to the President and his fellow members, and explain what is required of him as a member, and what the privileges are. If he is selected to play in the Pennant or other Association competition his obligation in "treating" his opponents must be explained; and he should be informed as to the weekly contribution during the Pennant and electric light seasons for spoons, etc.

A locker should be provided for him in the clubhouse.

If the new member has played before, his nominator should have the first game with him; but should he be a newcomer to the game, he should be handed over to the club coach. Assuming he does not possess a set of bowls, the coach should find the size of his hand by testing it on the Henselite Bowl Size Indicator and advising him as to the correct size and weight of bowl to use.

Excuses for bad play by bowlers should not be advanced. Good bowlers play poor games occasionally; when beaten, they do not blame the condition of the green, or the fact that the match was played off the ordinary setting of the rink — their victors had the same conditions to contend with. It is also bad form to bewail one's luck — generally the better bowler has the better luck. In any case luck does not always run against a bowler. It may for a while, but later on it will change.

However, it is better not to reckon on luck, but to depend upon one's own ability.

If you are selected to play for your club in a Pennant competition, remember you are playing for your club, and not for yourself. If the other Fours are up, and yours is down a few, do your best to score, but don't play risky shots, for the adverse outcome of them may turn an apparently certain win into a defeat.

MARKERS AND UMPIRES

If you are drawn to play in a Singles on a neutral green, but find it necessary from any cause to give a walkover, Etiquette requires that you notify the player (either direct or through his club) and the club on whose green you were to play, so that the Marker appointed for your match play may be released.

In any Club Singles (Championship, President's Prize, Century, Novice Handicap, and so on) be ready to do your share of marking — don't let "George" do it all. Marking is to be done for you; you should do it for others.

If the Marker does not come up to requirements, it may have been a poor performance, but he probably did his best. If he is marking a match in which a friend is playing, the Marker must be absolutely impartial, must not applaud any shot, must not wriggle his body as the bowl of his friend wicks in or just misses a trail, or give any advice to either player, excepting to answer question accurately and concisely. And when you have won the match, do not fail to thank the Marker for his service and to invite him in for a refresher, for an hour and a half of standing under a hot sun evaporates considerable moisture from the body, which requires replacement.

THE UMPIRE

If the Umpire is called in to decide a measure or any question, dispute, or difference which may arise in the course of a match and he decides against you, Etiquette demands that like the good sportsman you are, you must accept his decision.

If not satisfied with it and you decide to appeal to the controlling body, the Laws of the Game and Etiquette require that you must immediately inform the Umpire of the intention to appeal.

SPECTATORS

Persons not engaged in a match have their obligations. First of all they are required by the Regulations to preserve an attitude of stict neutrality. Difficult indeed in the case of partisans; but whilst they are within their rights in applauding good shots, it is definitely bad form for advice to be given by them to a player.

Spectators are not allowed on the green, and in fact, to comply with the Regulations, they should not be within three feet of the face of the bank.

Players should confine themselves to the match, and not mingle with the spectators or converse too freely with them.

DISTRACTING ATTENTION

It is not only against the Laws of the Game, but is contrary to Etiquette to attempt to distract the attention of the player on the mat as he is about to bowl. This distraction may be caused by talking loudly to the player, or to others so that the player may hear what is said.

The distraction can also result from over-loud remarks by bankers; and be caused by a deliberate (or an unintentional) movement by a player at the head. Sometimes the object is to interrupt the bowler's concentration. Gentlemen players do not wilfully do this sort of thing. The spirit of sportsmanship — and sportsmanship is Etiquette — is manliness and friendliness.

THE SUPERIORITY COMPLEX

A former prominent New Zealand player wrote, "I regret to notice that a number of experienced bowlers selfishly prefer to play among themselves." This action is not peculiar to New Zealand, but is a common and deplorable practice in many a club within the realm of Bowls. It is bad for the junior player, and is harmful to the club. The practice is the very opposite of Etiquette.

CLIQUISM

The friendliness of Bowls is not advanced by the tendency in some clubs towards cliquism. This inclination is hostile to the best interests of the club, opposed to the Etiquette of the game, and should be rigorously suppressed.

THERE'S A PLACE FOR EVERTHING

The throwing of dead matches etc. on the green or in the ditch is more a matter of lack of thought than of deliberate intention. Many a good bowl has been deflected in its running by contact with a match stick which a thoughtless smoker dropped on the green. That smoker must have had a box of matches in his hand at the time and the dead stick should have been put in the match box or in the container of the bank. The same may be said of cigarette butts, cigar ends, etc.

Of the insignificant few who expectorate on the green or in the ditch, the less said about them and this digusting habit the better. As the Greenkeeper stated, "Those who expectorate on the green cannot 'expect to rate' as gentlemen".

A FRENCH VERSION OF ETIQUETTE

A French bowling journal "La France Bouliste", quoted by Paul Garcin, in his "Le Jeu de Boules", gives the following advice:—

Be correct on the bowling-green.

Be scrupulously punctual.

Respect the rules.

Respect the instructions given to you.

Respect the decisions of the umpire.

Be polite to your opponents.

Be careful of your language.

Be careful of your demeanour.

Say little.

Obey your captain.

Control your joy when you win.

Be able to "take it" when you lose.

Be a man, and behave like one.

Be convinced that you have carried off the best of victories is your opponent of today becomes your friend of tomorrow.

A MEETING

The correct mode of address is "Mr. Chairman and Gentlemen", or "Mr. Chairman, Ladies and Gentlemen". When there is a specially distinguished person present on the platform, it is quite correct to include him in the address, thus: "Mr. Chairman, 'Sir Andrew', Ladies and Gentlemen". If there are several distinguished persons present, it would be indiscreet to single out anyone, and absurd to include the lot; and so the better plan is to omit all, and open with the plain "Mr. Chairman, Ladies and Gentlemen."

With regard to the case where the President of the National Bowling Association, or the President of the Provincial Bowling Association, a Member of Parliament, the local Mayor, and such like, are present at a bowling function the president of a bowling body should be addressed after the chairman of the meeting; just as the mayor should receive precedence at a municipal function, and the Member of Parliament at a political meeting.

At a social evening given by a bowling club, and at which toasts are to be proposed, the first toast should be that of "The Queen". It should be proposed by the president of the club, and before the toast is drunk, the National Anthem should be sung, all (with the exception of the pianist) standing to attention. The drinking of the toast then follows. No speech is made to this toast, and there is no response to it. The next toast should be that of "The Controlling Body"; and this should also be proposed by the president of the club, and later on the chief official of the Controlling Body present should make the response.

THE PRESIDENT AND HIS OFFICERS

Respect should be paid to the President, who, for the term of his appointment, is the head of the club, the chief of the clan.

The path he treads is generally not a smooth one; and he should not be worried by stones placed in his way — the petty differences that arise between members, who, in the interests of the harmony for which bowling clubs are noted, should resolve their disputes by a little give and take, and a hearty handshake. The President is made happy and encouraged when he knows that the harmony of the members is everything that could be desired.

The President, too, has his acts of Etiquette to perform by welcoming visitors to the club, in meeting new members and making them feel "at home". "Democracy, and not autocracy", should be ever his motto.

And similarly with the Immediate Past President and the Vice-Presidents. They should be backing the President solidly

— just as the Immediate Past was backed, and the Vice-Presidents expect to be.

Then there is the Hon. Secretary. He is the factotum of the club, and the honorarium he receives is usually inadequate recompense for the time and work he devotes to the club. Etiquette demands that he should have the kind thoughts and the willing help of the members. The courtesy he shows to them should be heartily reciprocated.

The work of the Hon. Treasurer can be made more pleasant by the prompt payment of subscriptions, competition fees, levies, and so on.

The Committeemen, as such, were elected to assist in the management of the club. They should be receptive to suggestions and constructive criticism by those not in office. Etiquette prefers that to destructive efforts.

In his capacity as a liaison between the Committee of Managements and the Green-keeper, the Green Director has an important job, and good Etiquette requires that any complaint by a player as to the condition of the green or the conduct of the Greenkeeper must be made to the Director and not to the Secretary or anyone else.

Now for the Selectors. They can make or break the harmony of the club. But if they select the teams on the merits of the players, and not because they themselves are on friendly terms with "Tom, Dick, or Harry", a de-graded player would not have a kick. It it is necessary to omit a usually good player from a team, or to put him in a lower one, it is good Etiquette for the Chairman of the Selection Committee to explain that as the player is out of form, it is obvious that in the interest of the success of the team he is reluctantly being displaced until he regains his former competency, and it is equally good Etiquette for the player to accept the position.

THE ETIQUETTE OF MARKING IN LAWN BOWLS

By

The Late John A. MALAN

(Former Life Member of The Royal Victorian Bowls
Association)

So if you would a Marker be
Then make it worth your while
To do the job quite capably
And do it with a smile.

—★—

PSYCHOLOGY OF BOWLING

Bowls is a science, the study of a lifetime, in which you may
exhaust yourself, but never your subject. It's a contest, a duel
calling for courage, skills, strategy and self-control. It is a test
of temper, a trial of honour, a revealer of character. It affords
the chance to play the man and act the gentleman. It means
going into God's out-of-doors, getting close to nature, fresh
air, exercise! A sweeping away of mental cobwebs, genuine
reaction of the tired tissues.

It is a cure for care, an antidote to worry. It includes com-
panionship with friends, social intercourse, opportunities for
courtesy, kindliness and generosity to an opponent. It promotes
not only physical health but moral force.

THE ETIQUETTE OF MARKING

A good marker is not only an asset to a club, but he adds
considerably to the enjoyment of the game by players and spectators alike, and the pity of it is that there are so few about.

COURTESY

It is not sufficiently appreciated that a singles match is essentially an elimination contest in which the players take the game

178

seriously and therefore the marker should likewise accept and perform his duties in a serious manner. The game requries the players to exercise their maximum powers of concentration, and all they ask from a marker is his undivided attention, which should be given firstly as a matter of courtesy, secondly as an interesting study of the individual player's capabilities, and thirdly because it provides an opportunity for learning more about the game even if it be only what not to do.

STUDY

A good marker, in whom the players have complete confidence, materially contributes to the quality of their game. It is a much mistaken notion that anyone can undertake the duties. No novice should ever volunteer to mark a game until he is completely versed in the duties of a marker, as set out in the Laws, and even then not until he has carefully studied other markers and their actions. In the closing stages of an Association event, when markers are carefully selected, the novice will do well to particularly study these officials.

EXPERIENCE

A marker should be an experienced bowler and a good judge of distance. "Experienced" does not mean a very good bowler, as there are excellent markers who have never been first-class bowlers, but they have had experience in the game and have found the job a pleasant and interesting one, as it undoubtedly is.

Far too many markers are distracted by the spectators and their comments, but could they "hear" the thoughts of the players they would quickly realise where their "reputations" were going. In matches, other than club events, a marker is virtually "wished" upon the players, and his efficiency, or lack of it, becomes a reflection on the club management, for, to the players, the marker IS the club for the time being. This aspect is one that club officials should remember, and should not hesitate to decline the services of non-competent volunteers.

The minimum requirement of a marker is that he shall know the duties as set out in the Laws, but few there be that fulfil even this standard. Fewer still are definite on what is meant by "jack high", yet the Laws contain an official definition,

179

which clearly states what is meant in answer to this very frequent question.

Before proceeding to the Head End the Marker should extend the hand of friendship to both players and make himself fully conversant with the ownership of the respective bowls. Certainly, in Association events and at least in club finals, the Marker should pay a compliment to the contestants by being correctly attired according to the Laws.

LOCATION

Before aligning the jack he should check whether the mat has been correctly laid. He should then retire to the position indicated in the Laws, until the first bowl has been delivered, and, during its course, proceed to alter the score board (if at that end) returning to his position in time to observe whether the bowl becomes a toucher. If possible a spectator should be asked to manipulate the score board, in which case he should be instructed not to do so during the period a player is on the mat prior to making a delivery. The exact position for a marker to stand is purposely not stated in the Laws, but the usual and generally acceptable position is from two to three metres (approximately 6 to 8 feet) behind the jack and two metres (approximately 6 feet) to one side, depending on the location of his shadow. Any extensive increase in these distances is undersirable as it involves a greater delay in answering a question.

A marker should remain motionless at his chosen spot with his attention and eyes fixed on the player whose turn it is to bowl so as to observe whether a question is asked, as quite frequently the question is not expressed in words, but in an action, such as holding an arm up indicating the question: "Am I the shot?" The marker's reply can then be given silently by an action (up or down) and in so doing no information is necessarily disclosed to the opponent unless he happens to observe the actions. In general a good marker is able to anticipate a likely question as the result of his own experience, plus the fact that he is sufficiently close to the head to know the position.

A marker must not move from his position except to observe whether a bowl is likely to become a toucher or to answer a question requiring a closer inspection. Under no circumstances whatsoever must he move, even by simply leaning over or turning sideways, to observe the head in order to satisfy his own curiosity or to anticipate a possible question. To move in any way is definitely contravening a Law as it gives an indication to the players of a possible change in the position that is not apparent to them. A marker must realise that the resultant effect of a bowl is not his concern, and any personal interest he may have in a player must not be shown. A biased marker is an anathema.

CONCENTRATION

It is somewhat surprising that so many players ask so few questions during a match and yet on reaching the head are so frequently heard to remark on the position being different from what they thought. Even if players have every confidence in their marker they become reluctant to ask a question if it involves a walk to the head by the marker because of the time delay in getting an answer. Therefore it is very essential for the marker to be alert and adjacent to the head.

The only player entitled to ask a question is the one whose turn it is to bowl, but he does not necessarily have to be standing on the mat, as some markers seem to think. One other point that every marker should always remember is that an inefficient marker can frequently be justifiably blamed, by the loser, for the result of the game, and that is something to be avoided at all costs.

DON'TS

In conclusion, this brief treatise would be incomplete without setting out a few of the major "Don'ts" to be observed—

(1) Don't answer questions that are being asked in an adjacent rink. Concentration and attention to the man on the mat will prevent this happening.

(2) Don't say the shot is doubtful if it is not really so. Experience at judging distances is something that can be acquired by anyone, provided they will indulge in a little practice on their own. It is most disconcerting to be told it is "up and down" and then find your opponent is at least one or more without even a measure.

(3) Don't forget to immediately advise the player if a bowl falls over and alters the position after a question has been

answered or an inspection of the head has been made by the player.

(4) Don't give a misleading answer to a badly-worded question. A marker is entitled to ask the player to re-state or clarify his question to enable an intelligent answer to be given. This particularly applies to such a question as: "Am I one down?" when he may be three down and to answer "Yes" or "No" is equally correct and incorrect, such a question is definitely a badly worded one. The proper form is: "Am I more than one down?" or "How many down am I?"

(5) Don't supplement your answer with information not asked for. Remember, every answer is common to both players and the questioner may not wish to gratuitously give information to his opponent. For instance, if asked to indicate which bowl is third shot, do so, but do **not** say whose bowl it is, or if asked whether the player is lying second shot, just say "Yes" or "No", but do **not** add that he is also third shot or some such similar information. The game provides ample scope for players to indulge in tactics to outwit each other, and the marker must be careful not to nullify their efforts.

(6) Arrange with the players before the match commences when they prefer touchers to be marked. The general practice is to mark a toucher immediately it has come to rest.

(7) Don't forget **HOW** to measure, as distinct from what to measure with. If you suspect A's bowl to be the nearer one, measure that first and then transfer to B's bowl, but on no account give an immediate decision, even if the answer be obvious. It is essential that the distance be transferred back to A's bowl so as to be quite sure that no movement has occurred. In the case of a really close measure, or where the players have previously measured, and a tie is a possibility, it is wise to repeat, at least once, the foregoing procedure before giving a decision. Immediately you have satisfied yourself as to the shot bowl, the best way to announce it is to move the winning bowl so that there can be no misunderstanding. Apart from satisfying the contestants it is just as important that the spectators shall have witnessed a proper judgment.

(8) Don't, under any circumstances, suggest or invite a player to inspect the head. To do so implies inability to give a satisfactory answer.

AN ART

If good marking be not a science, it is at least an art that can be acquired by any bowler who has the desire to become proficient, and in so doing he will not only be increasing his own enjoyment of the game, but will be contributing substantially to the enjoyment of the players and spectators alike.

A MARKER'S OPPORTUNITY

In the previous remarks on Etiquette, three reasons were given as to why a Marker should concentrate on the game and players to the complete exclusion of any attention to the spectators. The only permissible exception to this is during the crossover when it is customary to advise spectators and score board attendants by holding up the number of fingers indicating the shots scored. The hand to hold up is the one on the same side of the scoreboard as the player's name who won the end.

The first reason, that of courtesy to the players, need not be further emphasised, but the second reason, that of studying an individual's capabilities, warrants expansion. There is ample opportunity to do this, but many Markers fail to avail themselves of it, preferring to either chat with spectators or sit on the bank or even do both of these objectionable things from a player's point of view.

OBSERVATION

Probably the first conclusion that a regular Marker will arrive at is that the winner of a given game is not necessarily the better player. This deduction is one that emerges from the fact that in so many ways the fortunes of the game can be adverse for one player and favour the other. A bowl that falls over against its bias, a lucky shot that was not even attempted, a puff of wind, or some irregularity in the green are some of many fortuitous circumstances that come readily to mind. All of which add up to the fact that it is not entirely without justification that it has been described as an unfair game. Not that any lover of the game would have it otherwise, these hazards help to provide the enjoyment, and what is more enjoyable than to have a victory over an admittedly better player — such events are not exceptional.

JUDGMENT

So we come to the first important lesson for a Marker to learn, that the capabilities of a player must not be judged by the result alone. Therefore, he must look elsewhere if he wishes to honestly assess the ability of a player. The points upon which he should concentrate his attention are the delivery — is it smooth or does it wobble — is any attempt made to correct an error, of green or length, even an over correction indicates that the player knows his mistake — what type of shot is attempted, independent of the actual result, and bearing in mind that the head probably looks very different to the player — the occasions on which a question is asked and, equally important, the way it is asked as well as what is asked for. All these, together with other individual characteristics, will enable an observant Marker to reasonably assess the relative abilities of the two players. The opportunity thus provided is an almost compelling reason why, in club competitions, those who undertake the duty of a selector should avail themselves of every occasion presented to them of acting as a Marker.

UNDERSTANDING

As for the third reason given, that of learning more about the game, this again is a matter requring concentrated attention. To one who is a card player an understanding of the game of bowls is relatively simple on account of a similarity of combinations. The actual playing of a card is simple and, so, basically, is the delivery of a bowl. The correct card to play in a given set of circumstances requires experience that can only be obtained over a considerable period of time. Likewise the type of shot to play requires experience quite apart from the "know-how" of its delivery. There is virtually an infinitely unlimited number of card combinations and no hand or arrangement of associated hands ever repeat themselves. Likewise in bowls, there have never been two heads exactly alike although there are frequent repetitions of similar situations requiring virtually the same type of shot. Even identical circumstances can be dealt with in more than one way and in determining the best shot to play, it requires not only the ability of the player himself but an assessment of the probabilities of error and the potentialities of the opponent.

184

ADVANTAGE

And that brings us back to the importance of studying the players for whom you have the honour to be their Marker. It is particularly important in your own club events because it is certain that sooner or later one, if not both, will be your own opponent. With the knowledge you can gain now, it could just give you sufficient advantage to win, even against someone you admit is generally a better player than yourself. The winning of such a game supplies a greater thrill and more lasting pleasure than any other type of play.

So make the most of the opportunity you are now enjoying.

A MARKER'S DUTIES

The game of lawn bowls has acquired a recognised international status, nevertheless, complete uniformity in the Laws does not exist. However, the general broad framework of all the various codes, within which the nature of the game is identified, are sufficiently alike to warrant acceptance by the International Bowls Board. This Board has its own set of laws and many national authorities adopt them in toto. Others use a set that is regarded by them as being more complete and/or better suited for their local conditions. This particularly applies to Australia, South Africa and New Zealand, although they are all members of the I.B.B.

VARIATIONS

It would serve no good purpose to set out in detail the precise requirements of any or all of the various duties of a Marker. Even if they were to be given there is always the possibility of an alteration being made which would render the information either misleading or entirely wrong. Therefore, it becomes essential for a Marker to make himself familiar with the particular code under which a game is being conducted, as well as any special local conditions governing the compeition.

It might well be stressed that an international competition could be played under a set of laws that did not apply to the country in which the games are being played. However, in such a case the onus of providing a Marker with a copy of the exact duties expected of him then becomes the responsibility of the host country.

UNIFORMITY

Fortunately, many of the routine duties required are common to all codes and there is virtually no likelihood of them being varied so they can safely be listed as follows:—

Assisting to straighten the mat.

Aligning the jack.

Marking a toucher, or removing a prior chalk mark.

Removing a dead bowl.

Replacing a disturbance caused by himself.

Answering questions of fact.

Recording the score.

Advising the players of each progress score.

Seeing that the score board is correct.

Handling the completed and signed score card to the proper authority.

In addition, the Marker must never forget that the main purpose for his presence is to assist the players to enjoy the game, as well as to facilitate the actual play, by only answering the questions asked by the player next entitled to bowl. This should be done quickly and accurately so as to avoid the necessity of the players having to make a personal inspection of the head.

MARKER AS UMPIRE

It may so happen that a Marker is requested to also be the Umpire, and in some codes even his normal status is automatically virtually that of an Umpire. In either case it becomes imperative that he be well versed in the more comprehensive and important duties of this official. Under these circumstances he would be wise to have with him a copy of the applicable laws.

STATUS

The status of a Marker and/or an Umpire varies considerably according to the code of laws that are applicable. In some, their duties are determined on the basic principle that under no circumstances are players permitted to disregard any law and therefore these officials are vested with initiative status. This enables them to intervene at any time should they observe any breach. This principle stems from the usual authority of similarly placed officials in other forms of sport which generally involve some degree of public support, particularly on an international level.

The opposite attitude is that Bowls is in no way similar to other games, it being essentially a participants' recreation, with little or no public appeal beyond the bowling fraternity. In this case, the players themselves are morally bound to observe the laws, but should a breach be mutually condoned then no official has any authority to intervene. These officials have a potential status which only becomes operative if a player requests their services. In this school of thought it is felt that the basic object of a match (excluding its personal enjoyment) is to determine a winner and therefore it is entirely a matter for the players to decide the precise manner in which the result is achieved. This can obviously vary from a walk-over, or forfeit, to the meticulous application of every law. Any form of initiative status of an official would be construed as an intrusion on the players' personal enjoyment of the game.

CONCLUSION

The differences between initiative and potential status are by no means rigidly observed in the various codes, as several contain something of both in a kind of compromise. The Marker may have the right to prevent the playing to an under-length distance to the jack, whereas in other codes he may be expected to check the width of the rink and other matter-of-fact details which are usually left to the authority in charge of the green and are, therefore, taken for granted. Such variations may also apply to an Umpire. However, in any case the handy whereabouts of suitable measuring devices, etc., should be ascertained.

From what has been set out it will be realised that a Marker's services involve a thorough understanding of the game and the applicable code of laws and therefore the position should not be undertaken in a lighthearted manner.

There would appear to be little likelihood of a complete international uniformity of duties and status until the fundamentally divergent points of view have been satisfactorily resolved.

NOBODY'S DARLING
Up and down, walking, walking,
Often measuring, sometimes chalking.
Shifting mats — keeping score,
Thirty ends — may be more;
Aching back — tired of limb,
Cheers for others — none for him.
Night draws on, darker, darker,
No one cares for he's the MARKER.

187

THE ROMANCE OF BOWL MANUFACTURE
By
The Late J. P. MUNRO
(Noted Bowls Historian and former Hon. Secretary of the
Royal Victorian Bowls Association)

Are you wondering why we used the word "Romance"? Do you think that kind of word seems out of place associated with something prosaic like "Manufacture"? It's the right word! This is a story along classical lines — a story of triumph, of initiative, persistence and skill, of devotion to a cause. This is a story with no ending, but one that without an ending has brought happiness, enjoyment and relaxation to hundreds of thousands of people throughout the world. Unless this story could be written, the magnificent game of bowls, despite its rich tradition in history, would without doubt still be outside the grasp of the greater proportion of those to whom it has come to mean so much. This is a "Romance" right enough, a story of a success that has earned the gratitude of the whole international bowling fraternity.

Nobody knows when the era of wooden (lignum-vitae) bowls began in England, but it goes back many centuries. The island of San Domingo in the West Indies (where lignum-vitae comes from) was discovered by Columbus on December 3rd, 1492, so it is definite that the timber was unknown in England at that time. Lignum-vitae was introduced to Europe by the Spaniards in 1508, and it was probably brought to England by Sir Francis Drake either from the West Indies direct, or after being taken from the cargo of Spanish ships captured by him. Drake had equipped his ship, "The Pasha", with bowls and quoits for the recreation of his crew whilst resting on an island in the Gulf of Darien. Most probably the bowls were of lignum-vitae, and made by his ship's carpenters whilst waiting in the harbour at Plymouth during preparation for the voyage.

However, lignum-vitae became the popular timber for bowls manufacture in England and Scotland, by such makers as John Jacques & Son (established 1795), Thomas Taylor (1796),

Peter Boardman & Sons (1850), William Lindop (1855), R. G. Lawrie Ltd., F. H. Ayres Ltd., Bussey & Co. Ltd., the Taylor-Rolph Co., Slazengers Ltd., and others. Several of these firms still produce wooden bowls, although in recent years there has been a change in manufacture to composition bowls. The conversion of players in the British Isles from wooden bowls to composition bowls is a gradual but inevitable process. It has been recently estimated by a leading authority in England that the majority of wooden bowls will disappear from the greens in the next decade.

Bowling was first introduced in Australia when the early colonists, who had learn the art of bowling in England brought bowls with them. They played on a green built alongside the Beach Tavern at Sandy Bay, Hobart, in 1844. Perhaps there was something wrong with the concept of making a bowling-green an adjunct to a bar, rather than a bar an adjunct to a green, because hotel greens which were equipped with imported wooden bowls appeared and disappeared in some numbers between 1844 and 1864. It might be said that bowling as an established sport really commenced in Australia when, in 1864, Alcock & Co., Russell Street, Melbourne, turned several sets of lawn bowls from lignum-vitae skittle bowls for the newly formed Melbourne Bowling Club.

In 1867, at Parramatta, New South Wales, Thomas Eddes turned for Alexander Johnstone the first set of bowls used in New South Wales. In 1869 David Johnston was in business as a bowls manufacturer at 29 Latrobe Street, Melbourne, and on the opposite side, at 34 Latrobe Street, E. C. Johnston, a billiard table maker, included bowl manufacturing as one of his activities.

English and Scottish makes of lignum-vitae bowls continued to be used in Australia until the first decade of this century, when a few sets of composition bowls, imported from England, appeared on the greens. The material and shape of the bowl was unsatisfactory, and consequently they were not popular on the Australian greens.

About this time the sport began to feel the impact of a man destined to radically revolutionise the game of bowls — the man who, without doubt, Sir Francis Drake would select from everybody associated with the game as his First Mate — William David Hensell. He was to be associated with the

THE LATE WILLIAM D. HENSELL
1882—1959

development work in bowls manufacture for a brilliant 61 years — the period during which bowls became a fully matured internationally accepted sport.

William David Hensell was born in Richmond, Victoria, on January 2nd, 1882, and was educated at the Albert Park State School. At the age of 16 he was apprenticed to the wood-turning trade, but two years later (in 1900 to be exact) he transferred to Alcock & Co., billiard table manufacturers, then located in Russell Street, Melbourne. There he was taught the art of turning billiard balls, his tutor being Mr. W. J. Wood, who was a bowler and later on, the official bowls tester under Alcock & Co., who had been appointed by the Victorian Bowling Association on August 21st, 1901. Young Hensell was diligent and eager to learn, and his skill in turning the billiard balls was to help him later on when the turning and re-shaping of wooden bowls came into his hands. The game of bowls was making headway in Australia, but the wooden bowls then used were not stable, and they frequently required re-testing and re-biasing, particularly as a minimum bias bowl had been adopted by the Victorian Bowling Association.

Alcock & Co., of Melbourne, were appointed official testers to the Western Australian Bowling Association in 1902, and young Hensell was sent to Perth to do the testing, and there he remained for nearly seven years. It was during this formative period, without doubt, that his plans, later to revolutionise bowls production and the game itself, took their embryonic form.

Testing in those days was very primitive when the methods and equipment used today are considered. The equipment consisted of an ordinary billiard table, twelve feet long, with a wooden chute about two feet in length, with sufficient elevation to propel the bowl nine feet along the testing table, the slate bed of which was covered with billiard cloth only. The table gave only a crude indication of the bias of the bowl; and this caused quite a lot of concern because some bowls drew well on the green, but failed to pass the test for bias on the table, and vice versa.

In 1908 Alcock & Co., who were also the official testers for the New South Wales Bowling Association, lost the services of their tester, and the company transferred W. D. Hensell from Perth to Sydney. There he developed the first 36-foot testing-table, which was a big improvement on the 12-foot table, but it was still not perfect. Because of climatic conditions the wooden bowls shrunk out of their round shape, causing them to wobble, and to run very inconsistently when played on the green and when tested on the table. Realising that the obvious way to correct these bowls was to re-shape them, W. D. Hensell designed and perfected the first Australian machine to successfully re-shape shrunken and badly shaped bowls.

With this achievement, table testing became more of a success, but the technique of biasing and defective bowl correcting had still not been mastered, although considerable progress had been made in that direction. Bowlers could not appreciate the difficulties that at that time militated against good bowling. There, certainly, was the incentive and the opportunity for William Hensell to do something positive and constructive.

The battle against inaccuracy hadn't yet been won, but W. D. Hensell had started the long struggle destined to ultimately produce today's modern accurate, precision-built Henselite bowl.

At this time many new composition materials were being tried; they were relatively stable and free from many of the disadvantages of lignum-vitae. W. D. Hensell spent most of his spare time studying literature in connection with compositions. Eventually he came to the conclusion that vulcanite (hard rubber) was the most suitable composition available at that time for bowl manufacture.

Returning to Melbourne in 1918, W. D. Hensell was fortunate to meet Mr. Roberts, Works Manager of Dunlop Rubber Co., a keen bowler, who had brought his wooden bowls along for re-testing. This was a grand opportunity to exploit the ideas he had conceived, and after he explained the many advantages a hard rubber bowl would have over wood, and the potential demand for such a bowl, Mr. Roberts became impressed and responsive to Mr. Hensell's enthusiasm. As a result, after many experiments a round Ebonite ball approximately 5'' diameter was produced, turned and made into a bowl.

When tested on the table, however, it was found to have an eccentric action, being heavier on one side, which caused it to be out of balance. Further experiments and more care produced twelve consistent rubber balls. They were turned into bowls — the twelve tested perfectly — AND RUBBER

BOWLS, THE FIRST IN THE WORLD, WERE BORN.

It was obvious that the concept of a hard rubber bowl had become a reality and that sufficient progress had been made to justify the making of moulds and equipment for the manufacture of these new bowls.

In June, 1918, Mr. Hensell terminated employment with Alcock & Co., to start a business of his own at 386 Little Bourke Street, Melbourne, where he had fitted up the latest and most reliable testing-table and turning plant. Little did he imagine when he was so busy building his testing-table and acquiring plant, that he was on the threshold of a business career during which he would achieve his ultimate ambition — that of making the best bowl in the world, "Henselite", and being the largest manufacturer of lawn bowls.

The Dunlop Rubber Co. made arrangements with Mr. W. D. Hensell to turn, bias, and finish all their rubber bowls, after the company had moulded them. Before the end of 1918 the first vulcanite or ebonite bowls in the world were being used — and with success — on Victorian greens. Their advent created considerable interest and started a controversy as to the merits of the two types of bowl — the wooden and the composition. However, bowlers soon realised the many advantages of the composition bowl, and a change-over took place almost immediately, many leading players seeing fit to discard their old woods for the new rubbers. During the period from 1918 to 1924 the rubber bowl became so popular that the importation into Australia of lignum-vitae (wooden) bowls completely ceased, and Australia became an exporter of bowls.

In the early days of rubber bowls many problems had to be solved. Causing major concern was internal variation in the specific gravity of the rubber compound. This made it difficult to obtain the exact required weight for each size of bowl. The solution to the problem was to "load" the core of each bowl to the required weight and then cover it with a high quality ebonite.

As the game grew in popularity so did W. D. Hensell's business, and larger premises were necessary. Moves were made first to 347 Elizabeth Street, Melbourne, then to 9 Cobden Street, North Melbourne, and in 1937 to the present location at 16-22 Wreckyn Street, North Melbourne. These premises have since been enlarged, more adjacent properties bought, and in 1960 an additional storey was built on to the original building to provide a large modern suite of offices as well as to expand production area.

Further properties were bought and new showrooms, offices and warehouses built in 1979 which allowed for further expansion of the production area and the Australian distribution of other sporting goods.

To achieve greater accuracy in the biasing of rubber bowls, it became necessary to revise many of the table-testing ideas. Improvements were made to the testing chutes, and the bed of the table was covered with a special billard rubber, and a canvas, to give the same speed as that of a good running bowling green. With these improvements bowls could now be tested for both bias and balance (a new development which proved to be the most revolutionary innovation ever adopted for table testing). For the first time bowls could be accurately tested on the table under conditions similar to playing conditions on a green, whether fast or slow.

Contrary to the belief of many bowlers — and particularly those of the younger generation — the bias of a bowl is not brought about by extra weight on one side of the bowl, but by the shape of the crown or running surface, which is slightly higher on the non-bias side.

The faster a bowl is delivered the straighter it will run. As a bowl loses momentum, because of the shape of its crown, the bowl gradually changes its running surface, and the bias takes effect. Eventually it reaches its maximum draw as the bowl slows down and comes to rest.

Many modifications to the shape and crown of the bowl were made until it was improved to such an extent that it was more comfortable to hold than the old-fashioned wooden bowl. With these improvements the death knell of the old wooden bowl was sounded in Australia, as the performance of the new bowl was far superior.

The Australian Bowling Council's Laws of the Game then in force, permitted a maximum weight of (3 lbs. 8 ozs.) (1.6kg) irrespective of the size of the bowl. Bowlers were quick to take advantage of the improvement in bowls and soon realised they could successfully use a much smaller bowl of heavier weight. With the old wooden bowl, if a reasonable weight were required, bowlers had to procure a large "pudding shape" set, which were too big for comfortable delivery or for reasonable control.

The Australian Bowling Council acted quickly and in 1922 appointed a bowls testing committee of four (Messrs. E. W. Walker, J. B. Grut, W. Barr of Victoria, and A. Moore, of Queensland), with Mr. W. D. Hensell as Technical Adviser, to thoroughly investigate this matter along with other problems. After months of experiments and tests carried out under various conditions on both tables and greens of all speeds, the committee made recommendations to the Council specifying bowls of standard shape, and a scale of maximum weights for each size. They also determined the minimum bias suitable for Australian conditions.

The Council approved, and the new scale of weights and measures came into operation on January 3rd, 1926. Although the reforms seemed very drastic, a standard had been set, which was adopted by the New Zealand Bowling Association in 1938, and by the International Bowling Board in 1946 in a modified form to suit climatic conditions. It is obvious now that these reforms were based on broad understanding and vision; they were exactly what were required to stabilise the situation.

(In 1962, the International Bowling Board specified that the maximum weight of a bowl shall be 3lb. 8oz. (1.6kg.) and the A.B.C. amended its laws accordingly — reverting to the original weight specified in force before 1926. The "maximum weight — per size" laws were eventually dispensed with in all countries, thus permitting the maximum weight of any size bowl to be 3lb. 8oz. (1.6kg.).)

By 1930 very few wooden bowls were seen on the greens in Australia, as rubber bowls, which were being constantly improved, had superseded them. They were being extensively used overseas, too, particularly in New Zealand and South Africa. At this time the Dunlop Rubber Co. made a decision that was indirectly and unintentionally designed to usher in a new era of bowls development. They decided to turn and finish, as well as mould, these rubber bowls in their own factory at Montague, Victoria. In all W. D. Hensell had turned and finished for them 13,750 sets of Dunlop bowls, and in addition many thousands of sets of all makes had been re-tested, re-conditioned, etc.

Consequently his arrangements with the Dunlop Co. were

terminated. His reaction was to conceive the idea of developing and making an entirely new bowl, ultimately to be named "HENSELITE".

For ten years, W. D. Hensell had been training his son, Ray, in the skilled art of bowl manufacturing, and it says a great deal for the courage and determination of father and son that the name of Hensell didn't become bowls history at this time.

They immediately became a two-man research team, working with the objective of producing a new bowl, incorporating improvements in design and performance, made of a composition superior to rubber, less affected by heat and climatic conditions. Ever foremost in their minds was the ambition that the new bowl must be solid throughout, without any core, wear-resistant, tough and durable. This was quite an objective — but the Hensells, it transpires, were capable of the task.

About this time the "Plastics Age" was gathering momentum, and the Hensells quickly learnt of a Sydney firm that had just started to manufacture a plastic material with the frightening name of Phenolformaldehyde moulding compound. Its properties were oustanding, and it promised to be the ideal material for which they were searching.

Initial inquiries were disappointing, as this material could only be moulded to a thickness of ½", whereas a solid moulding at least 5" in diameter and weighing 3½lbs (1.56kg) was required. Surely, they said, there must be some way to mould this material into bowls. Nobody could stop them that way! Someone had said much the same thing about rubber once.

Undaunted by early failures, they decided to continue experiments with the technical assistance of Dr. Lang, an authority on this type of plastic. New formulae and sample batches of material were made, different techniques tried and discarded. Eventually Dr. Lang perfected a special moulding compound, and from it the first solid one-piece plastic bowl was made — THE "HENSELITE" BOWL.

A new bowling era had commenced. History was made, not only in bowls manufacturing, but in the plastics industry, as manufacturers all over the world were astounded when the "Henselite" achievement became known. Even today it is believed that the plastic bowl is the largest solid mass of phenolformaldehyde compound moulded.

Plans were then prepared for the making of the intricate moulds and the installation of the necessary moulding plant to make the new bowls. Many difficulties and problems were encountered before it was possible to start manufacturing on a production basis. Perfection was eventually achieved, and in April, 1931, the first set of Henselite bowls was produced. When used on the green, they were acclaimed by everyone who tried them. It was obvious from this moment that the new bowl was outstanding in appearance and performance, and was superior in every respect to any other make of bowl.

At this time Australia was in the throes of a depression, and the name "Henselite" was new and almost unknown. Despite this, there was an immediate demand for these new bowls. They were available in black, mahogany and chocolate, with discs of several colours, making them most attractive.

The fame of "Henselite" rapidly grew. Top-line bowlers changed to "Henselite", and demonstrated their superiority by winning most of the important championships. Sales increased to such an extent that plant and production had to be enlarged to supply the demand.

Trial orders were sent to South Africa and the immediate reaction was astounding. Repeat orders soon followed. The demand for "Henselite" soon spread to the British Isles, New Zealand, Canada, U.S.A. and other countries. Regular shipments are now exported to the British Isles, South Africa, New Zealand, Canada, United States, Zimbabwe, Hong Kong, Japan, Fiji, Malaya, Kenya, New Guinea, Norfolk Island, South America, Israel and Holland. HENSELITE BOWLS PREDOMINATE IN EVERY COUNTRY WHERE BOWLS IS PLAYED.

More developments followed. Previously all bowls had inserted discs; these were liable to become loose, crack and fall out. In 1937 the "Henselite" Uni-Disc Bowl was introduced. This incorporated the discs as an integral part of the bowl. Engravings of initials or distinctive designs are engraved on the bowl and filled with lacquer of various colours. It was not long before this innovation was copied by other manufacturers.

In the same year the first "Henselite" all-white plastic jack was produced. Centreless ground to high precision, these jacks are perfectly round and have superseded the old china jack, which was irregular in shape, chipped easily and was generally

RAYMOND W. HENSELL
1906—1979

unsatisfactory. The moulding of these jacks from Urea Formaldehyde moulding powder was in itself an outstanding achievement.

After having spent 45 years perfecting the art of bowl testing, and pioneering the manufacture of bowls, W. D. Hensell retired from active business in 1944. The responsibility of management and the designing of new plant and equipment of sufficient capacity to cope with the postwar demand for bowls fell heavily on the shoulders of R. W. Hensell. He had made and installed an entirely new moulding plant to be used in conjunction with a new process of electronic pre-heating requiring elaborate and complex equipment and capable of high production.

A series of automatic high precision turning and biasing machines were also designed. When they were completed and installed, the production of bowls was resumed after the war years, on the 6th February, 1946. This new plant proved so successful that for the first time in the world it enabled the mass production of bowls more accurate than was ever before thought possible.

Mr. W. D. Hensell passed away at the age of 77 in August, 1959. The bowling world thus lost the services of a man responsible to a great degree for its growth and development. Prior to this R. W. Hensell's two sons became associated in the business, and the company of R. W. Hensell & Sons Pty. Ltd., was established.

In 1959 Ray Hensell again surprised the bowling fraternity by announcing a new "Henselite" Super Grip model. This was re-designed for improved performance, and as the result of new formulas, developed after extensive research, the moulding compound was impregnated with special additives to greatly improve the "grip", giving it a velvety "feel", particularly under wet and cold conditions. It also removes the necessity of frequent polishing. Now proved, this new model has been acclaimed as a further step forward in bowl perfection.

Constantly it has been a continuing story of more research, more plant, more production and more world-wide acclaim for a bowl that has given the game and its players such pleasure and satisfaction.

Climatic conditions, types of grass and green surfaces vary considerably in different countries. Consequently, special models of bowls are made to suit these conditions. In New Zealand, for instance, the greens are undoubtedly the fastest in the world, and windy conditions are common. As a result, the New Zealand model bowls have a flatter crown, with slightly less bias than Australian bowls. South African greens were usually hard and bumpy, and a special heavyweight bowl is used to suit these conditions. In the British Isles, greens are invariably wet, soft and heavy. To get the best results a lightweight model bowl is used. All models comply with the respective regulations of each bowling country.

This study of overseas bowling conditions is a constant one, and many overseas trips have been made to study bowling conditions in different countries and to ensure maximum performances of every "Henselite" model.

Most bowlers will be staggered to learn that, in order to supply bowls suitable for the different conditions existing in various countries, a total of 678 models of "Henselites" are made in numerous sizes, bias, shapes, weights and colours — excluding the several thousand different engravings covering a multitude of categories and colourings.

Over recent years the game of Indoor Bowls, in various forms, has met with increasing popularity, and "Henselite" Indoor Bowls are again foremost in demand for playing this rapidly growing game. The range of bowls manufactured has been extended to provide miniature carpet bowls, round indoor bowls, biased indoor bowls, as well as the bowl jacks to suit each type of game.

The sales story has been a spectacular one. When World War II started in 1939, annual sales had topped 4,000 sets. From 1942 to 1945 the whole plant was devoted to the war effort, and there was no production of bowls. After the war, new staff had to be completely trained, new modern plant was installed to allow potential production of 10,000 sets per annum. In 1946, 9,500 sets were produced. This production figure was well behind demand. With steady increase of plant and factory space, 15,000 sets were produced in 1947, and 20,000 in 1948. The story continues, with constant growth of the game itself, and expansion by R. W. Hensell & Sons Pty. Ltd. At the end of 1960, the production for the year exceeded 33,000 sets per annum. This, of course, is in lawn bowls only, and excluded the many thousands of sets of indoor types and jacks. More than 1,000,000 sets of "Henselite" bowls have now been

Fig. 23—The 750,000th set of Henselite Bowls, made on the 7th June, 1972, being checked on the Testing Table by Mr. R. W. Hensell and his sons, Bruce and Graeme.

produced using more than 6,500 tons of moulding compound, specially processed for the requirements of the various models of bowls.

The production figures are much higher than the output of all other bowl manufacturers in the world put together. To R. W. Hensell & Sons Pty. Ltd., must go the undisputed honour of being not only the largest manufacturer of bowls but of achieving the distinction of producing the world's best bowl.

Mr. R. W. Hensell retired from active business in 1976 and passed away at the age of 72 on 6th March, 1979.

A milestone in the history of "Henselite" bowls was celebrated on 13th March, 1980, when the 4,000,000th "Henselite" bowl (1 million sets) came through production. Now suitably mounted and proudly displayed, it perpetuates the hopes and fears, the toil and worry, the brilliance and the determination of the two men. William and Ray Hensell. It symbolises a game started by Sir Francis Drake or his contemporaries — something that has grown to be more than a game, more than a means of relaxation and pleasure. It represents a pursuit that has become a cement in the mixture of man and man — an influence towards peaceful co-existence between nations.

Australian industry regards "Henselite" with pride . . . they are setting a valuable example in exporting more than 50% of their production to 24 overseas countries — truly an excellent contribution to Australia's export trade for which the company received Australian Government "Awards for Outstanding Export Achievement" in 1963, 1972 and 1982.

An era was ushered in by William David Hensell and developed in the true Hensell fashion by Raymond William Hensell who brought precision into bowl manufacture to the ultimate of perfection.

Now there are two more Hensells, Bruce Raymond (Managing Director) and Graeme Westcott (Director) actively engaged in the business, now operating as Henselite (Australia) Pty. Ltd., and already in this "computer age", have brought automation and computerisation to bowls production and time will, no doubt, show us further new ideas they will develop — what further contribution the third generation of Hensells will make to our wonderful traditional old game — Bowls.

Mr. Bruce R. Hensell (right) receives Henselite (Aust) Pty. Ltd.'s third export award from former Minister for Commerce, Sir Philip Lynch (Photo — Canberra Times).

HENSELITE FIRSTS

1908 **First** full-sized testing table built.
1910 **First** turning machine made to reshape wooden bowls.
1918 **First** Rubber Bowl ever made.
1930 **First** Plastic Bowl manufactured.
1937 **First** all white Plastic Bowl Jack made.
1937 **First** to introduce Uni-disc Bowl.
1937 **First** to perfect balance testing of bowls.
1945 **First** Mass Production by automatic precision bowl turning and biasing machines.
1956 **First** Millionth Bowl made.
1959 **First** Super-Grip Model Bowl produced.
1962 **First** bowls manufacturer to receive Helms Foundation Award in recognition of noteworthy contributions to Lawn Bowling.
1963 **First** winner of Australian Government "Award for Outstanding Export Achievement".
1964 **First** manufacturer to produce 2,000,000 lawn bowls.
1966 **First** World Bowls Championships, Sydney — Gold Medal Winners in every event.
1967 **First** introduction of DeLuxe Model bowl.
1972 **First** manufacturer to produce 3,000,000 lawn bowls.
1972 **First** bowls manufacturer to win second Australian Government "Award for Outstanding Export Achievement".
1980 **First** manufacturer to produce 4,000,000 lawn bowls (1,000,000 sets).
1981 **First** to introduce Size 0 (4-5/8") lawn bowl.
1982 **First** bowls manufacturer to win third Australian Government "Award for Outstanding Export Achievement".